Turn About Eleanor

Ethel M. Kelley

Alpha Editions

This edition published in 2024

ISBN : 9789362519481

Design and Setting By
Alpha Editions
www.alphaedis.com
Email - info@alphaedis.com

Contents

CHAPTER I ....- 1 -

CHAPTER II ....- 7 -

CHAPTER III ....- 13 -

CHAPTER IV ....- 19 -

CHAPTER V ....- 23 -

CHAPTER VI ....- 30 -

CHAPTER VII ....- 34 -

CHAPTER VIII ....- 39 -

CHAPTER IX ....- 46 -

CHAPTER X ....- 51 -

CHAPTER XI ....- 56 -

CHAPTER XII ....- 63 -

CHAPTER XIII ....- 72 -

CHAPTER XIV ....- 76 -

CHAPTER XV ....- 83 -

CHAPTER XVI ....- 89 -

CHAPTER XVII ....- 93 -

CHAPTER XVIII ....- 101 -

CHAPTER XIX ....- 109 -

CHAPTER XX ....- 117 -

CHAPTER XXI ....- 122 -

CHAPTER XXII ....- 127 -

CHAPTER XXIII ....- 132 -

CHAPTER XXIV ....- 137 -

CHAPTER XXV ....- 143 -

CHAPTER I

A child in a faded tam-o'-shanter that had once been baby blue, and a shoddy coat of a glaring, unpropitious newness, was sitting uncomfortably on the edge of a hansom seat, and gazing soberly out at the traffic of Fifth Avenue.

The young man beside her, a blond, sleek, narrow-headed youth in eye-glasses, was literally making conversation with her. That is, he was engaged in a palpable effort to make conversation—to manufacture out of the thin crisp air of that November morning and the random impressions of their progress up the Avenue, something with a general resemblance to tête-à-tête dialogue as he understood it. He was succeeding only indifferently.

"See, Eleanor," he pointed brightly with his stick to the flower shop they were passing, "see that building with the red roof, and all those window boxes. Don't you think those little trees in pots outside look like Christmas trees? Sometimes when your Aunts Beulah and Margaret and Gertrude, whom you haven't met yet—though you are on your way to meet them, you know—sometimes when they have been very good, almost good enough to deserve it, I stop by that little flower shop and buy a chaste half dozen of gardenias and their accessories, and divide them among the three."

"Do you?" the child asked, without wistfulness. She was a good child, David Bolling decided,—a sporting child, willing evidently to play when it was her turn, even when she didn't understand the game at all. It was certainly a new kind of game that she would be so soon expected to play her part in,—a rather serious kind of game, if you chose to look at it that way.

David himself hardly knew how to look at it. He was naturally a conservative young man, who had been brought up by his mother to behave as simply as possible on all occasions, and to avoid the conspicuous as tacitly and tactfully as one avoids a new disease germ. His native point of view, however, had been somewhat deflected by his associations. His intimate circle consisted of a set of people who indorsed his mother's decalogue only under protest, and with the most stringent reservations. That is, they were young and healthy, and somewhat overcharged with animal spirits, and their reactions were all very intense and emphatic.

He was trying at this instant to look rather more as if he were likely to meet one of his own friends than one of his mother's. His mother's friends would not have understood his personal chaperonage of the shabby little girl at his elbow. Her hair was not even properly brushed. It looked frazzled and tangled; and at the corner of one of her big blue eyes, streaking diagonally across the pallor in which it was set, was a line of dirt,—a tear mark, it might have been, though that didn't make the general effect any less untidy, David thought; only a trifle more uncomfortably pathetic. She was a nice little girl, that fact was becoming more and more apparent to David, but any friend of his mother's would have wondered, and expressed him or herself as wondering, why in the name of all sensitiveness he had not taken a taxicab, or at least something in the nature of a closed vehicle, if he felt himself bound to deliver in person this curious little stranger to whatever mysterious destination she was for.

"I thought you'd like a hansom, Eleanor, better than a taxi-cab, because you can see more. You've never been in this part of New York before, I understand."

"No, sir."

"You came up from Colhassett last Saturday, didn't you? Mrs. O'Farrel wrote to your grandmother to send you on to us, and you took the Saturday night boat from Fall River."

"Yes, sir."

"Did you travel alone, Eleanor?"

"A friend of Grandpa's came up on the train with me, and left me on the vessel. He told the colored lady and gentleman to see if I was all right,—Mr. Porter and Mrs. Steward."

"And were you all right?" David's eyes twinkled.

"Yes, sir."

"Not sea sick, nor homesick?"

The child's fine-featured face quivered for a second, then set again into impassive stoic lines, and left David wondering whether he had witnessed a vibration of real emotion, or the spasmodic twitching of the muscles that is so characteristic of the rural public school.

"I wasn't sea sick."

"Tell me about your grandparents, Eleanor." Then as she did not respond, he repeated a little sharply, "Tell me about your grandparents, won't you?"

The child still hesitated. David bowed to the wife of a Standard Oil director in a passing limousine, and one of the season's prettiest débutantes, who was walking; and because he was only twenty-four, and his mother was very, very ambitious for him, he wondered if the tear smudge on the face of his companion had been evident from the sidewalk, and decided that it must have been.

"I don't know how to tell," the child said at last, "I don't know what you want me to say."

"I don't want you to say anything in particular, just in general, you know."

David stuck. The violet eyes were widening with misery, there was no doubt about it. "Game, clean through," he said to himself. Aloud he continued. "Well, you know, Eleanor.—Never say 'Well,' if you can possibly avoid it, because it's a flagrant Americanism, and when you travel in foreign parts you're sure to regret it,—well, you know, if you are to be in a measure my ward—and you are, my dear, as well as the ward of your Aunts Beulah and Margaret and Gertrude, and your Uncles Jimmie and Peter—I ought to begin by knowing a little something of your antecedents. That is why I suggested that you tell me about your grandparents. I don't care what you tell me, but I think it would be very suitable for you to tell me something. Are they native Cape Codders? I'm a New Englander myself, you know, so you may be perfectly frank with me."

"They're not summer folks," the child said. "They just live in Colhassett all the year round. They live in a big white house on the depot road, but they're so old now, they can't keep it up. If it was painted it would be a real pretty house."

"Your grandparents are not very well off then?"

The child colored. "They've got lots of things," she said, "that Grandfather brought home when he went to sea, but it was Uncle Amos that sent them the money they lived on. When he died they didn't have any."

"How long has he been dead?"

"Two years ago Christmas."

"You must have had some money since then."

"Not since Uncle Amos died, except for the rent of the barn, and the pasture land, and a few things like that."

"You must have had money put away."

"No," the little girl answered. "We didn't. We didn't have any money, except what came in the way I said. We sold some old-fashioned dishes, and a little bit of cranberry bog for twenty-five dollars. We didn't have any other money."

"But you must have had something to live on. You can't make bricks without straw, or grow little girls up without nourishing food in their tummies." He caught an unexpected flicker of an eyelash, and realized for the first time that the child was acutely aware of every word he was saying, that even his use of

English was registering a poignant impression on her consciousness. The thought strangely embarrassed him. "We say tummies in New York, Eleanor," he explained hastily. "It's done here. The New England stomick, however, is almost entirely obsolete. You'll really get on better in the circles to which you are so soon to be accustomed if you refer to it in my own simple fashion;—but to return to our muttons, Eleanor, which is French for getting down to cases, again, you must have had something to live on after your uncle died. You are alive now. That would almost seem to prove my contention."

"We didn't have any money, but what I earned."

"But—what you earned. What do you mean, Eleanor?"

The child's face turned crimson, then white again. This time there was no mistaking the wave of sensitive emotion that swept over it.

"I worked out," she said. "I made a dollar and a half a week running errands, and taking care of a sick lady vacations, and nights after school. Grandma had that shock, and Grandpa's back troubled him. He tried to get work but he couldn't. He did all he could taking care of Grandma, and tending the garden. They hated to have me work out, but there was nobody else to."

"A family of three can't live on a dollar and a half a week."

"Yes, sir, they can, if they manage."

"Where were your neighbors all this time, Eleanor? You don't mean to tell me that the good, kindly people of Cape Cod would have stood by and let a little girl like you support a family alone and unaided. It's preposterous."

"The neighbors didn't know. They thought Uncle Amos left us something. Lots of Cape Cod children work out. They thought that I did it because I wanted to."

"I see," said David gravely.

The wheel of their cab became entangled in that of a smart delivery wagon. He watched it thoughtfully. Then he took off his glasses, and polished them.

"Through a glass darkly," he explained a little thickly. He was really a very *young* young man, and once below the surface of what he was pleased to believe a very worldly and cynical manner, he had a profound depth of tenderness and human sympathy.

Then as they jogged on through the Fifty-ninth Street end of the Park, looking strangely seared and bereft from the first blight of the frost, he turned to her again. This time his tone was as serious as her own.

"Why did you stop working out, Eleanor?" he asked.

"The lady I was tending died. There wasn't nobody else who wanted me. Mrs. O'Farrel was a relation of hers, and when she came to the funeral, I told her that I wanted to get work in New York if I could,—and then last week she wrote me that the best she could do was to get me this place to be adopted, and so—I came."

"But your grandparents?" David asked, and realized almost as he spoke that he had his finger on the spring of the tragedy.

"They had to take help from the town."

The child made a brave struggle with her tears, and David looked away quickly. He knew something of the temper of the steel of the New England nature; the fierce and terrible pride that is bred in the bone of the race. He knew that the child before him had tasted of the bitter waters of humiliation in seeing her kindred "helped" by the town. "Going out to work," he understood, had brought the family pride low, but taking help from the town had leveled it to the dust.

"There is, you know, a small salary that goes with this being adopted business," he remarked casually a few seconds later. "Your Aunts Gertrude and Beulah and Margaret, and your three stalwart uncles aforesaid, are not the kind of people who have been brought up to expect something for nothing. They don't expect to adopt a perfectly good orphan without money and without price, merely for the privilege of experimentation. No, indeed, an orphan in good standing of the best New England extraction ought to exact for her services a salary of at least fifteen dollars a month. I wouldn't consent to take a cent less, Eleanor."

"Wouldn't you?" the child asked uncertainly. She sat suddenly erect, as if an actual burden had been dropped from her shoulders. Her eyes were not violet, David decided, he had been deceived by the depth of their coloring; they were blue, Mediterranean blue, and her lashes were an inch and a half long at the very least. She was not only pretty, she was going to be beautiful some day. A strange premonition struck David of a future in which this long-lashed, stoic baby was in some way inextricably bound.

"How old are you?" he asked her abruptly.

"Ten years old day before yesterday."

They had been making their way through the Park; the searer, yellower Park of late November. It looked duller and more cheerless than David ever remembered it. The leaves rattled on the trees, and the sun went down suddenly.

"This is Central Park," he said. "In the spring it's very beautiful here, and all the people you know go motoring or driving in the afternoon."

He bowed to his mother's milliner in a little French runabout. The Frenchman stared frankly at the baby blue tam-o'-shanter and the tangled golden head it surmounted.

"Joseph could make you a peachy tam-o'-shanter looking thing of blue velvet; I'll bet I could draw him a picture to copy. Your Uncle David, you know, is an artist of a sort."

For the first time since their incongruous association began the child met his smile; her face relaxed ever so little, and the lips quivered, but she smiled a shy, little dawning smile. There was trust in it and confidence. David put out his hand to pat hers, but thought better of it.

"Eleanor," he said, "my mother knows our only living Ex-president, and the Countess of Warwick, one Vanderbilt, two Astors, and she's met Sir Gilbert Parker, and Rudyard Kipling. She also knows many of the stars and satellites of upper Fifth Avenue. She has, as well, family connections of so much weight and stolidity that their very approach, singly or in conjunction, shakes the earth underneath them.—I wish we could meet them all, Eleanor, every blessed one of them."

CHAPTER II

THE COOPERATIVE PARENTS

"I wonder how a place like this apartment will look to her," Beulah said thoughtfully. "I wonder if it will seem elegant, or cramped to death. I wonder if she will take to it kindly, or with an ill concealed contempt for its limitations."

"The poor little thing will probably be so frightened and homesick by the time David gets her here, that she won't know what kind of a place she's arrived at," Gertrude suggested. "Oh, I wouldn't be in your shoes for the next few days for anything in the world, Beulah Page; would you, Margaret?"

The third girl in the group smiled.

"I don't know," she said thoughtfully. "It would be rather fun to begin it."

"I'd rather have her for the first two months, and get it over with," Beulah said decisively. "It'll be hanging over your head long after my ordeal is over, and by the time I have to have her again she'll be absolutely in training. You don't come until the fifth on the list you know, Gertrude. Jimmie has her after me, then Margaret, then Peter, and you, and David, if he has got up the courage to tell his mother by that time."

"But if he hasn't," Gertrude suggested.

"He can work it out for himself. He's got to take the child two months like the rest of us. He's agreed to."

"He will," Margaret said, "I've never known him to go back on his word yet."

"Trust Margaret to stick up for David. Anyway, I've taken the precaution to put it in writing, as you know, and the document is filed."

"We're not adopting this infant legally."

"No, Gertrude, we can't,—yet, but morally we are. She isn't an infant, she's ten years old. I wish you girls would take the matter a little more seriously. We've bound ourselves to be responsible for this child's whole future. We have undertaken her moral, social and religious education. Her body and soul are to be—"

"Equally divided among us," Gertrude cut in.

Beulah scorned the interruption.

"—held sacredly in trust by the six of us, severally and collectively."

"Why haven't we adopted her legally then?" Margaret asked.

"Well, you see, there are practical objections. You have to be a corporation or an institution or something, to adopt a child as a group. A child can't have three sets of parents in the eyes of the law, especially when none of them is married, or have the least intention of being married, to each other.—I don't see what you want to keep laughing at, Gertrude. It's all a little unusual and modern and that sort of thing, but I don't think it's funny. Do you, Margaret?"

"I think that it's funny, but I think that it's serious, too, Beulah."

"I don't see what's funny about—" Beulah began hotly.

"You don't see what's funny about anything,—even Rogers College, do you, darling? It is funny though for the bunch of us to undertake the upbringing of a child ten years old; to make ourselves financially and spiritually responsible for it. It's a lot more than funny, I know, but it doesn't seem to me as if I could go on with it at all, until somebody was willing to admit what a *scream* the whole thing is."

"We'll admit that, if that's all you want, won't we, Beulah?" Margaret appealed.

"If I've got this insatiable sense of humor, let's indulge it by all means," Gertrude laughed. "Go on, chillun, go on, I'll try to be good now."

"I wish you would," Margaret said. "Confine yourself to a syncopated chortle while I get a few facts out of Beulah. I did most of my voting on this proposition by proxy, while I was having the measles in quarantine. Beulah, did I understand you to say you got hold of your victim through Mrs. O'Farrel, your seamstress?"

"Yes, when we decided we'd do this, we thought we'd get a child about six. We couldn't have her any younger, because there would be bottles, and expert feeding, and well, you know, all those things. We couldn't have done it, especially the boys. We thought six would be just about the right age, but we simply couldn't find a child that would do. We had to know about its antecedents. We looked through the orphan asylums, but there wasn't anything pure-blooded American that we could be sure of. We were all agreed that we wanted pure American blood. I knew Mrs. O'Farrel had relatives on Cape Cod. You know what that stock is, a good sea-faring strain, and a race of wonderfully fine women, 'atavistic aristocrats' I remember an author in the *Atlantic Monthly* called them once. I suppose you think it's funny to groan, Gertrude, when anybody makes a literary allusion, but it isn't. Well, anyway, Mrs. O'Farrel knew about this child, and sent for her. She stayed with Mrs. O'Farrel over Sunday, and now David is bringing her here. She'll be here in a minute."

"Why David?" Gertrude twinkled.

"Why not David?" Beulah retorted. "It will be a good experience for him, besides David is so amusing when he tries to be, I thought he could divert her on the way."

"It isn't such a crazy idea, after all, Gertrude." Margaret Hutchinson was the youngest of the three, being within several months of her majority, but she looked older. Her face had that look of wisdom that comes to the young who have suffered physical pain. "We've got to do something. We're all too full of energy and spirits, at least the rest of you are, and I'm getting huskier every minute, to twirl our hands and do nothing. None of us ever wants to be married,—that's settled; but we do want to be useful. We're a united group of the closest kind of friends, bound by the ties of—of—natural selection, and we need a purpose in life. Gertrude's a real artist, but the rest of us are not, and—and—"

"What could be more natural for us than to want the living clay to work on? That's the idea, isn't it?" Gertrude said. "I can be serious if I want to, Beulah-land, but, honestly, girls, when I come to face out the proposition, I'm almost afraid to. What'll I do with that child when it comes to be my turn? What'll Jimmie do? Buy her a string of pearls, and show her the night life of New York very likely. How'll I break it to my mother? That's the cheerful little echo in my thoughts night and day. How did you break it to yours, Beulah?"

Beulah flushed. Her serious brown eyes, deep brown with wine-colored lights in them, met those of each of her friends in turn. Then she laughed.

"Well, I do know this is funny," she said, "but, you know, I haven't dared tell her. She'll be away for a month, anyway. Aunt Ann is here, but I'm only telling her that I'm having a little girl from the country to visit me."

Occasionally the architect of an apartment on the upper west side of New York—by pure accident, it would seem, since the general run of such apartments is so uncomfortable, and unfriendly—hits upon a plan for a group of rooms that are at once graciously proportioned and charmingly convenient, while not being an absolute offense to the eye in respect to the details of their decoration. Beulah Page and her mother lived in such an apartment, and they had managed with a few ancestral household gods, and a good many carefully related modern additions to them, to make of their eight rooms and bath, to say nothing of the ubiquitous butler's-pantry, something very remarkably resembling a home, in its most delightful connotation: and it was in the drawing room of this home that the three girls were gathered.

Beulah, the younger daughter of a widowed mother—now visiting in the home of the elder daughter, Beulah's sister Agatha, in the expectation of what the Victorians refer to as an "interesting event"—was technically under the chaperonage of her Aunt Ann, a solemn little spinster with no control whatever over the movements of her determined young niece.

Beulah was just out of college,—just out, in fact, of the most high-minded of all the colleges for women;—that founded by Andrew Rogers in the year of our Lord eighteen hundred and sixty-one. There is probably a greater percentage of purposeful young women graduated from Rogers College every year, than from any other one of the communities of learning devoted to the education of women; and of all the purposeful classes turned out from that admirable institution, Beulah's class could without exaggeration be designated as the most purposeful class of them all. That Beulah was not the most purposeful member of her class merely argues that an almost abnormally high standard of purposefulness was maintained by practically every individual in it.

At Rogers every graduating class has its fad; its propaganda for a crusade against the most startling evils of the world. One year, the sacred outlines of the human figure are protected against disfigurement by an ardent group of young classicists in Grecian draperies. The next, a fierce young brood of vegetarians challenge a lethargic world to mortal combat over an Argentine sirloin. The year of Beulah's graduation, the new theories of child culture that were gaining serious headway in academic circles, had filtered into the class rooms, and Beulah's mates had contracted the contagion instantly. The entire senior class went mad on the subject of child psychology and the various scientific prescriptions for the direction of the young idea.

It was therefore primarily to Beulah Page, that little Eleanor Hamlin, of Colhassett, Massachusetts, owed the change in her fortune. At least it was to Beulah that she owed the initial inspiration that set the wheel of that fortune in motion; but it was to the glorious enterprise and idealism of youth, and the courage of a set of the most intrepid and quixotic convictions that ever quickened in the breasts of a mad half dozen youngsters, that she owed the actual fulfillment of her adventure.

The sound of the door-bell brought the three girls to their feet, but the footfalls in the corridor, double quick time, and accentuated, announced merely the arrival of Jimmie Sears, and Peter Stuyvesant, nicknamed *Gramercy* by common consent.

"Has she come?" Peter asked.

But Jimmie struck an attitude in the middle of the floor.

"My daughter, oh! my daughter," he cried. "This suspense is killing me. For the love of Mike, children, where is she?"

"She's coming," Beulah answered; "David's bringing her."

Gertrude pushed him into the *chaise-lounge* already in the possession of Margaret, and squeezed in between them.

"Hold my hand, Jimmie," she said. "The feelings of a father are nothing,— *nothing* in comparison to those which smolder in the maternal breast. Look at Beulah, how white she is, and Margaret is trembling this minute."

"I'm trembling, too," Peter said, "or if I'm not trembling, I'm frightened."

"We're all frightened," Margaret said, "but we're game."

The door-bell rang again.

"There they come," Beulah said, "oh! everybody be good to me."

The familiar figure of their good friend David appeared on the threshold at this instant, and beside him an odd-looking little figure in a shoddy cloth coat, and a faded blue tam-o'-shanter. There was a long smudge of dirt reaching from the corner of her eye well down into the middle of her cheek. A kind of composite gasp went up from the waiting group, a gasp of surprise, consternation, and panic. Not one of the five could have told at that instant what it was he expected to see, or how his imagination of the child differed from the concrete reality, but amazement and keen disappointment constrained them. Here was no figure of romance and delight. No miniature Galatea half hewn out of the block of humanity, waiting for the chisel of a composite Pygmalion. Here was only a grubby, little unkempt child, like all other children, but not so presentable.

"What's the matter with everybody?" said David with unnatural sharpness. "I want to present you to our ward, Miss Eleanor Hamlin, who has come a long way for the pleasure of meeting you. Eleanor, these are your cooperative parents."

The child's set gaze followed his gesture obediently. David took the little hand in his, and led the owner into the heart of the group. Beulah stepped forward.

"This is your Aunt Beulah, Eleanor, of whom I've been telling you."

"I'm pleased to make your acquaintance, Aunt Beulah," the little girl said, as Beulah put out her hand, still uncertainly.

Then the five saw a strange thing happen. The immaculate, inscrutable David—the aristocrat of aristocrats, the one undemonstrative, super-self-conscious member of the crowd, who had been delegated to transport the little orphan chiefly because the errand was so incongruous a mission on which to despatch him—David put his arm around the neck of the child with a quick protecting gesture, and then gathered her close in his arms, where she clung, quivering and sobbing, the unkempt curls straggling helplessly over his shoulder.

He strode across the room where Margaret was still sitting upright in the *chaise-lounge*, her dove-gray eyes wide, her lips parted.

"Here, you take her," he said, without ceremony, and slipped his burden into her arms.

"Welcome to our city, Kiddo," Jimmie said in his throat, but nobody heard him.

Peter, whose habit it was to walk up and down endlessly wherever he felt most at home, paused in his peregrination, as Margaret shyly gathered the rough little head to her bosom. The child met his gaze as he did so.

"We weren't quite up to scratch," he said gravely.

Beulah's eyes filled. "Peter," she said, "Peter, I didn't mean to be—not to be—"

But Peter seemed not to know she was speaking. The child's eyes still held him, and he stood gazing down at her, his handsome head thrown slightly back; his face deeply intent; his eyes softened.

"I'm your Uncle Peter, Eleanor," he said, and bent down till his lips touched her forehead.

CHAPTER III

Eleanor walked over to the steam pipes, and examined them carefully. The terrible rattling noise had stopped, as had also the choking and gurgling that had kept her awake because it was so like the noise that Mrs. O'Farrel's aunt, the sick lady she had helped to take care of, made constantly for the last two weeks of her life. Whenever there was a sound that was anything like that, Eleanor could not help shivering. She had never seen steam pipes before. When Beulah had shown her the room where she was to sleep—a room all in blue, baby blue, and pink roses—Eleanor thought that the silver pipes standing upright in the corner were a part of some musical instrument, like a pipe organ. When the rattling sound had begun she thought that some one had come into the room with her, and was tuning it. She had drawn the pink silk puff closely about her ears, and tried not to be frightened. Trying not to be frightened was the way she had spent a good deal of her time since her Uncle Amos died, and she had had to look out for her grandparents.

Now that it was morning, and the bright sun was streaming into the windows, she ventured to climb out of bed and approach the uncanny instrument. She tripped on the trailing folds of that nightgown her Aunt Beulah—it was funny that all these ladies should call themselves her aunts, when they were really no relation to her—had insisted on her wearing. Her own nightdress had been left in the time-worn carpetbag that Uncle David had forgotten to take out of the "handsome cab." She stumbled against the silver pipes. They were *hot*; so hot that the flesh of her arm nearly blistered, but she did not cry out. Here was another mysterious problem of the kind that New York presented at every turn, to be silently accepted, and dealt with.

Her mother and father had once lived in New York. Her father had been born here, in a house with a brownstone front on West Tenth Street, wherever that was. She herself had lived in New York when she was a baby, though she had been born in her grandfather's house in Colhassett. She had lived in Cincinnati, Ohio, too, until she was four years old, and her father and mother had died there, both in the same week, of pneumonia. She wished this morning, that she could remember the house where they lived in New York, and the things that were in it.

There was a knock on the door. Ought she to go and open the door in her nightdress? Ought she to call out "Come in?" It might be a gentleman, and her Aunt Beulah's nightdress was not very thick. She decided to cough, so that whoever was outside might understand she was in there, and had heard them.

"May I come in, Eleanor?" Beulah's voice called.

"Yes, ma'am." She started to get into bed, but Miss—Miss—the nearer she was to her, the harder it was to call her aunt,—Aunt Beulah might think it was time she was up. She compromised by sitting down in a chair.

Beulah had passed a practically sleepless night working out the theory of Eleanor's development. The six had agreed on a certain sketchily defined method of procedure. That is, they were to read certain books indicated by Beulah, and to follow the general schedule that she was to work out and adapt to the individual needs of the child herself, during the first phase of the experiment. She felt that she had managed the reception badly, that she had not done or said the right thing. Peter's attitude had shown that he felt the situation had been clumsily handled, and it was she who was responsible for it. Peter was too kind to criticize her, but she had vowed in the muffled depths of a feverish pillow that there should be no more flagrant flaws in the conduct of the campaign.

"Did you sleep well, Eleanor?" she asked.

"Yes, ma'am."

"Are you hungry?"

"No, ma'am."

The conversation languished at this.

"Have you had your bath?"

"I didn't know I was to have one."

"Nice little girls have a bath every day."

"Do they?" Eleanor asked. Her Aunt Beulah seemed to expect her to say something more, but she couldn't think of anything.

"I'll draw your bath for you this morning. After this you will be expected to take it yourself."

Eleanor had seen bathrooms before, but she had never been in a bath-tub. At her grandfather's, she had taken her Saturday night baths in an old wooden wash-tub, which had water poured in it from the tea kettle. When Beulah closed the door on her she stepped gingerly into the tub: the water was twice too hot, but she didn't know how to turn the faucet, or whether she was expected to turn it. Mrs. O'Farrel had told her that people had to pay for water in New York. Perhaps Aunt Beulah had drawn all the water she could have. She used the soap sparingly. Soap was expensive, she knew. She wished there was some way of discovering just how much of things she was expected to use. The number of towels distressed her, but she finally took the littlest and dried herself. The heat of the water had nearly parboiled her.

After that, she tried to do blindly what she was told. There was a girl in a black dress and white apron that passed her everything she had to eat. Her Aunt Beulah told her to help herself to sugar and to cream for her oatmeal, from off this girl's tray. Her hand trembled a good deal, but she was fortunate enough not to spill any. After breakfast she was sent to wash her hands in the bathroom; she turned the faucet, and used a very little water. Then, when she was called, she went into the sitting-room and sat down, and folded her hands in her lap.

Beulah looked at her with some perplexity. The child was docile and willing, but she seemed unexpectedly stupid for a girl ten years old.

"Have you ever been examined for adenoids, Eleanor?" she asked suddenly.

"No, ma'am."

"Say, 'no, Aunt Beulah.' Don't say, 'no, ma'am' and 'yes, ma'am.' People don't say 'no, ma'am' and 'yes, ma'am' any more, you know. They say 'no' and 'yes,' and then mention the name of the person to whom they are speaking."

"Yes, ma'am," Eleanor couldn't stop herself saying it. She wanted to correct herself. "No, Aunt Beulah, no, Aunt Beulah," but the words stuck in her throat.

"Well, try to remember," Beulah said. She was thinking of the case in a book of psychology that she had been reading that morning, of a girl who was "pale and sleepy looking, expressionless of face, careless of her personal appearance," who after an operation for adenoids, had become "as animated and bright as before she had been lethargic and dull." She was pleased to see that Eleanor's fine hair had been scrupulously combed, and neatly braided this morning, not being able to realize—as how should she?—that the condition of Eleanor's fine spun locks on her arrival the night before, had been attributable to the fact that the O'Farrel baby had stolen her comb, and Eleanor had been too shy to mention the fact, and had combed her hair mermaid-wise, through her fingers.

"This morning," Beulah began brightly, "I am going to turn you loose in the apartment, and let you do what you like. I want to get an idea of the things you do like, you know. You can sew, or read, or drum on the piano, or talk to me, anything that pleases you most. I want you to be happy, that's all, and to enjoy yourself in your own way."

"Give the child absolute freedom in which to demonstrate the worth and value of its ego,"—that was what she was doing, "keeping it carefully under observation while you determine the individual trend along which to guide its development."

The little girl looked about her helplessly. The room was very large and bright. The walls were white, and so was the woodwork, the mantle, and some of the furniture. Gay figured curtains hung at the windows, and there were little stools, and chairs, and even trays with glass over them, covered with the same bright colored material. Eleanor had never seen a room anything like it. There was no center-table, no crayon portraits of different members of the family, no easels, or scarves thrown over the corners of the pictures. There were not many pictures, and those that there were didn't seem to Eleanor like pictures at all, they were all so blurry and smudgy,— excepting one of a beautiful lady. She would have liked to have asked the name of that lady,—but her Aunt Beulah's eyes were upon her. She slipped down from her chair and walked across the room to the window.

"Well, dear, what would make this the happiest day you can think of?" Beulah asked, in the tone she was given to use when she asked Gertrude and Margaret and Jimmie—but not often Peter—what they expected to do with their lives.

Eleanor turned a desperate face from the window, from the row of bland elegant apartment buildings she had been contemplating with unseeing eyes.

"Do I have to?" she asked Beulah piteously.

"Have to what?"

"Have to amuse myself in my own way? I don't know what you want me to do. I don't know what you think that I ought to do."

A strong-minded and spoiled younger daughter of a widowed mother— whose chief anxiety had been to anticipate the wants of her children before they were expressed—with an independent income, and a beloved and admiring circle of intimate friends, is not likely to be imaginatively equipped to explore the spiritual fastnesses of a sensitive and alien orphan. Beulah tried earnestly to get some perspective on the child's point of view, but she could not. The fact that she was torturing the child would have been outside of the limits of her comprehension. She searched her mind for some immediate application of the methods of Madame Montessori, and produced a lump of modeling clay.

"You don't really have to do anything, Eleanor," she said kindly. "I don't want you to make an effort to please me, only to be happy yourself. Why don't you try and see what you can do with this modeling clay? Just try making it up into mud pies, or anything."

"Mud pies?"

"Let the child teach himself the significance of contour, and the use of his hands, by fashioning the clay into rudimentary forms of beauty." That was the theory.

"Yes, dear, mud pies, if you wish to."

Whereupon Eleanor, conscientiously and miserably, turned out a neat half-dozen skilful, miniature models of the New England deep dish apple-pie, pricked and pinched to a nicety.

Beulah, with a vision related to the nebulous stages of a study by Rodin, was somewhat disconcerted with this result, but she brightened as she thought at least she had discovered a natural tendency in the child that she could help her develop.

"Do you like to cook, Eleanor?" she asked.

In the child's mind there rose the picture of her grim apprenticeship on Cape Cod. She could see the querulous invalid in the sick chair, her face distorted with pain and impatience; she could feel the sticky dough in her fingers, and the heat from the stove rising round her.

"I hate cooking," she said, with the first hint of passion she had shown in her relation to her new friends.

The day dragged on wearily. Beulah took her to walk on the Drive, but as far as she was able to determine the child saw nothing of her surroundings. The crowds of trimly dressed people, the nursemaids and babies, the swift slim outlines of the whizzing motors, even the battleships lying so suggestively quiescent on the river before them—all the spectacular, vivid panorama of afternoon on Riverside Drive—seemed absolutely without interest or savor to the child. Beulah's despair and chagrin were increasing almost as rapidly as Eleanor's.

Late in the afternoon Beulah suggested a nap. "I'll sit here and read for a few minutes," she said, as she tucked Eleanor under the covers. Then, since she was quite desperate for subjects of conversation, and still determined by the hot memory of her night's vigil to leave no stone of geniality unturned, she added:

"This is a book that I am reading to help me to know how to guide and educate you. I haven't had much experience in adopting children, you know, Eleanor, and when there is anything in this world that you don't know, there is usually some good and useful book that will help you to find out all about it."

Even to herself her words sounded hatefully patronizing and pedagogic, but she was past the point of believing that she could handle the situation with grace. When Eleanor's breath seemed to be coming regularly, she put down her book with some thankfulness and escaped to the tea table, where she poured tea for her aunt, and explained the child's idiosyncrasies swiftly and smoothly to that estimable lady.

Left alone, Eleanor lay still for a while, staring at the design of pink roses on the blue wall-paper. On Cape Cod, pink and blue were not considered to be colors that could be combined. There was nothing at all in New York like anything she knew or remembered. She sighed. Then she made her way to the window and picked up the book Beulah had been reading. It was about *her*, Aunt Beulah had said,—directions for educating her and training her. The paragraph that caught her eye where the book was open had been marked with a pencil.

"This girl had such a fat, frog like expression of face," Eleanor read, "that her neighbors thought her an idiot. She was found to be the victim of a severe case of ad-e-noids." As she spelled out the word, she recognized it as the one Beulah had used earlier in the day. She remembered the sudden sharp look with which the question had been accompanied. The sick lady for whom she had "worked out" had often called her an idiot when her feet had stumbled, or she had failed to understand at once what was required of her.

Eleanor read on. She encountered a text replete with hideous examples of backward and deficient children, victims of adenoids who had been restored to a state of normality by the removal of the affliction. She had no idea what an adenoid was. She had a hazy notion that it was a kind of superfluous bone in the region of the breast, but her anguish was rooted in the fact that this, *this* was the good and useful book that her Aunt Beulah had found it necessary to resort to for guidance, in the case of her own—Eleanor's—education.

When Beulah, refreshed by a cup of tea and further sustained by the fact that Margaret and Peter had both telephoned they were coming to dinner, returned to her charge, she found the stolid, apathetic child she had left, sprawling face downward on the floor, in a passion of convulsive weeping.

CHAPTER IV

It was Peter who got at the heart of the trouble. Margaret tried, but though Eleanor clung to her and relaxed under the balm of her gentle caresses, the child remained entirely inarticulate until Peter gathered her up in his arms, and signed to the others that he wished to be left alone with her.

By the time he rejoined the two in the drawing-room—he had missed his after-dinner coffee in the long half-hour that he had spent shut into the guest room with the child—Jimmie and Gertrude had arrived, and the four sat grouped together to await his pronouncement.

"She thinks she has adenoids. She wants the doll that David left in that carpetbag of hers he forgot to take out of the 'Handsome cab.' She wants to be loved, and she wants to grow up and write poetry for the newspapers," he announced. "Also she will eat a piece of bread and butter and a glass of milk, as soon as it can conveniently be provided for her."

"When did you take holy orders, Gram?" Jimmie inquired. "How do you work the confessional? I wish I could make anybody give anything up to me, but I can't. Did you just go into that darkened chamber and say to the kid, 'Child of my adoption,—cough,' and she coughed, or are you the master of some subtler system of choking the truth out of 'em?"

"Anybody would tell anything to Peter if he happened to want to know it," Margaret said seriously. "Wouldn't they, Beulah?"

Beulah nodded. "She wants to be loved," Peter had said. It was so simple for some people to open their hearts and give out love,—easily, lightly. She was not made like that,—loving came hard with her, but when once she had given herself, it was done. Peter didn't know how hard she had tried to do right with the child that day.

"The doll is called the rabbit doll, though there is no reason why it should be, as it only looks the least tiny bit like a rabbit, and is a girl. Its other name is Gwendolyn, and it always goes to bed with her. Mrs. O'Farrels aunt said that children always stopped playing with dolls when they got to be as big as Eleanor, but she isn't never going to stop.—You must get after that double negative, Beulah.—She once wrote a poem beginning: 'The rabbit doll, it is my own.' She thinks that she has a frog-like expression of face, and that is why Beulah doesn't like her better. She is perfectly willing to have her adenoids cut out, if Beulah thinks it would improve her, but she doesn't want to 'take anything,' when she has it done."

"You are a wonder, Gram," Gertrude said admiringly.

"Oh! I have made a mess of it, haven't I?" Beulah said. "Is she homesick?"

"Yes, she's homesick," Peter said gravely, "but not for anything she's left in Colhassett. David told you the story, didn't he?—She is homesick for her own kind, for people she can really love, and she's never found any of them. Her grandfather and grandmother are old and decrepit. She feels a terrible responsibility for them, but she doesn't love them, not really. She's too hungry to love anybody until she finds the friends she can cling to—without compromise."

"An emotional aristocrat," Gertrude murmured. "It's the curse of taste."

"Help! Help!" Jimmie cried, grimacing at Gertrude. "Didn't she have any kids her own age to play with?"

"She had 'em, but she didn't have any time to play with them. You forget she was supporting a family all the time, Jimmie."

"By jove, I'd like to forget it."

"She had one friend named Albertina Weston that she used to run around with in school. Albertina also wrote poetry. They used to do poetic 'stunts' of one poem a day on some subject selected by Albertina. I think Albertina was a snob. She candidly admitted to Eleanor that if her clothes were more stylish, she would go round with her more. Eleanor seemed to think that was perfectly natural."

"How do you do it, Peter?" Jimmie besought. "If I could get one damsel, no matter how tender her years, to confide in me like that I'd be happy for life. It's nothing to you with those eyes, and that matinée forehead of yours; but I want 'em to weep down my neck, and I can't make 'em do it."

"Wait till you grow up, Jimmie, and then see what happens," Gertrude soothed him.

"Wait till it's your turn with our child," Margaret said. "In two months more she's coming to you."

"Do I ever forget it for a minute?" Jimmie cried.

"The point of the whole business is," Peter continued, "that we've got a human soul on our hands. We imported a kind of scientific plaything to exercise our spiritual muscle on, and we've got a real specimen of womanhood in embryo. I don't know whether the situation appalls you as much as it does me—" He broke off as he heard the bell ring.

"That's David, he said he was coming."

Then as David appeared laden with the lost carpetbag and a huge box of chocolates, he waved him to a chair, and took up his speech again. "I don't know whether the situation appalls you, as much as it does me—if I don't get this off my chest now, David, I can't do it at all—but the thought of that poor little waif in there and the struggle she's had, and the shy valiant spirit of her,—the sand that she's got, the *sand* that put her through and kept her mouth shut through experiences that might easily have killed her, why I feel as if I'd give anything I had in the world to make it up to her, and yet I'm not altogether sure that I could—that we could—that it's any of our business to try it."

"There's nobody else who will, if we don't," David said.

"That's it," Peter said, "I've never known any one of our bunch to quit anything that they once started in on, but just by way of formality there is one thing we ought to do about this proposition before we slide into it any further, and that is to agree that we want to go on with it, that we know what we're in for, and that we're game."

"We decided all that before we sent for the kid," Jimmie said, "didn't we?"

"We decided we'd adopt a child, but we didn't decide we'd adopt this one. Taking the responsibility of this one is the question before the house just at present."

"The idea being," David added, "that she's a fairly delicate piece of work, and as time advances she's going to be *delicater*."

"And that it's an awkward matter to play with souls," Beulah contributed; whereupon Jimmie murmured, "Browning," sotto voice.

"She may be all that you say, Gram," Jimmie said, after a few minutes of silence, "a thunderingly refined and high-minded young waif, but you will admit that without an interpreter of the same class, she hasn't been much good to us so far."

"Good lord, she isn't refined and high-minded," Peter said. "That's not the idea. She's simply supremely sensitive and full of the most pathetic possibilities. If we're going to undertake her we ought to realize fully what we're up against, and acknowledge it,—that's all I'm trying to say, and I apologize for assuming that it's more my business than anybody's to say it."

"That charming humility stuff, if I could only remember to pull it."

The sofa pillow that Gertrude aimed at Jimmie hit him full on the mouth and he busied himself pretending to eat it. Beulah scorned the interruption.

"Of course, we're going to undertake her," Beulah said. "We are signed up and it's all down in writing. If anybody has any objections, they can state them now." She looked about her dramatically. On every young face was reflected the same earnestness that set gravely on her own.

"The 'ayes' have it," Jimmie murmured. "From now on I become not only a parent, but a soul doctor." He rose, and tiptoed solemnly toward the door of Eleanor's room.

"Where are you going, Jimmie?" Beulah called, as he was disappearing around the bend in the corridor.

He turned back to lift an admonitory finger.

"Shush," he said, "do not interrupt me. I am going to wrap baby up in a blanket and bring her out to her mothers and fathers."

CHAPTER V

ELEANOR ENJOYS HERSELF IN HER OWN WAY

"I am in society here," Eleanor wrote to her friend Albertina, with a pardonable emphasis on that phase of her new existence that would appeal to the haughty ideals of Miss Weston, "I don't have to do any housework, or anything. I sleep under a pink silk bedquilt, and I have all new clothes. I have a new black pattern leather sailor hat that I sopose you would laugh at. It cost six dollars and draws the sun down to my head but I don't say anything. I have six aunts and uncles all diferent names and ages but grown up. Uncle Peter is the most elderly, he is twenty-five. I know becase we gave him a birthday party with a cake. I sat at the table. I wore my crape da shine dress. You would think that was pretty, well it is. There is a servant girl to do evry thing even passing your food to you on a tray. I wish you could come to visit me. I stay two months in a place and get broghut up there. Aunt Beulah is peculiar but nice when you know her. She is stric and at first I thought we was not going to get along. She thought I had adenoids and I thought she dislikt me too much, but it turned out not. I take lessons from her every morning like they give at Rogers College, not like publick school. I have to think what I want to do a good deal and then do it. At first she turned me loose to enjoy myself and I could not do it, but now we have disapline which makes it all right. My speling is weak, but uncle Peter says Stevanson could not spel and did not care. Stevanson was the poat who wrote the birdie with a yellow bill in the reader. I wish you would tel me if Grandma's eye is worse and what about Grandfather's rheumatism.

"Your fond friend, Eleanor.

"P. S. We have a silver organ in all the rooms to have heat in. I was afrayd of them at first."

In the letters to her grandparents, however, the undercurrent of anxiety about the old people, which was a ruling motive in her life, became apparent.

"Dear Grandma and Dear Grandpa," she wrote,

"I have been here a weak now. I inclose my salary, fifteen dollars ($15.00) which I hope you will like. I get it for doing evry thing I am told and being adoptid besides. You can tell the silectmen that I am rich now and can support you just as good as Uncle Amos. I want Grandpa to buy some heavy undershurts right of. He will get a couff if he doesn't do it. Tell him to rub your arm evry night before you go to bed, Grandma, and to have a hot soapstone for you. If you don't have your bed hot you will get newmonia and I can't come home to take care of you, becase my salary would stop. I like New York better now that I have lived here some. I miss seeing you around, and Grandpa.

"The cook cooks on a gas stove that is very funny. I asked her how it went and she showed me it. She is going to leve, but lucky thing the hired girl can cook till Aunt Beulah gets a nother cook as antyseptic as this cook. In Rogers College they teach ladies to have their cook's and hired girl's antyseptic. It is a good idear becase of sickness. I inclose a recipete for a good cake. You can make it sating down. You don't have to stir it much, and Grandpa can bring you the things. I will write soon. I hope you are all right. Let me hear that you are all right. Don't forget to put the cat out nights. I hope she is all right, but remember the time she stole the butter fish. I miss you, and I miss the cat around. Uncle David pays me my salary out of his own pocket, because he is the richest, but I like Uncle Peter the best. He is very handsome and we like to talk to each other the best. Goodbye, Eleanor."

But it was on the varicolored pages of a ruled tablet—with a picture on its cover of a pink cheeked young lady beneath a cherry tree, and marked in large straggling letters also varicolored "The Cherry Blossom Tablet"—that Eleanor put down her most sacred thoughts. On the outside, just above the cherry tree, her name was written with a pencil that had been many times wet to get the desired degree of blackness, "Eleanor Hamlin, Colhassett, Massachusetts. Private Dairy," and on the first page was this warning in the same painstaking, heavily shaded chirography, "This book is sacrid, and not be trespased in or read one word of. By order of owner. E. H."

It was the private diary and Gwendolyn, the rabbit doll, and a small blue china shepherdess given her by Albertina, that constituted Eleanor's *lares et penates*. When David had finally succeeded in tracing the ancient carpetbag in the lost and found department of the cab company, Eleanor was able to set up her household gods, and draw from them that measure of strength and security inseparable from their familiar presence. She always slept with two of the three beloved objects, and after Beulah had learned to understand and appreciate the child's need for unsupervised privacy, she divined that the little girl was happiest when she could devote at least an hour or two a day to the transcribing of earnest sentences on the pink, blue and yellow pages of the Cherry Blossom Tablet, and the mysterious games that she played with the rabbit doll. That these games consisted largely in making the rabbit doll impersonate Eleanor, while the child herself became in turn each one of the six uncles and aunts, and exhorted the victim accordingly, did not of course occur to Beulah. It did occur to her that the pink, blue and yellow pages would have made interesting reading to Eleanor's guardians, if they had been privileged to read all that was chronicled there.

"My aunt Beulah wears her hair to high of her forrid.

"My aunt Margaret wears her hair to slic on the sides.

"My aunt Gertrude wears her hair just about right.

"My aunt Margaret is the best looking, and has the nicest way.

"My aunt Gertrude is the funniest. I never laugh at what she says, but I have trouble not to. By thinking of Grandpa's rheumaticks I stop myself just in time. Aunt Beulah means all right, and wants to do right and have everybody else the same.

"Uncle David is not handsome, but good.

"Uncle Jimmie is not handsome, but his hair curls.

"Uncle Peter is the most handsome man that ere the sun shown on. That is poetry. He has beautiful teeth, and I like him.

"Yesterday the Wordsworth Club—that's what Uncle Jimmie calls us because he says we are seven—went to the Art Museum to edjucate me in art.

"Aunt Beulah wanted to take me to one room and keep me there until I asked to come out. Uncle Jimmie wanted to show me the statures. Uncle David said I ought to begin with the Ming period and work down to Art Newvoo. Aunts Gertrude and Margaret wanted to take me to the room of the great masters. While they were talking Uncle Peter and I went to see a picture that made me cry. I asked him who she was. He said that wasn't the important thing, that the important thing was that one man had nailed his dream. He didn't doubt that lots of other painters had, but this one meant the most to him. When I cried he said, 'You're all right, Baby. You know.' Then he reached down and kissed me."

As the month progressed, it seemed to Beulah that she was making distinct progress with the child. Since the evening when Peter had won Eleanor's confidence and explained her mental processes, her task had been illumined for her. She belonged to that class of women in whom maternity arouses late. She had not the facile sympathy which accepts a relationship without the endorsement of the understanding, and she was too young to have much toleration for that which was not perfectly clear to her.

She had started in with high courage to demonstrate the value of a sociological experiment. She hoped later, though these hopes she had so far kept to herself, to write, or at least to collaborate with some worthy educator, on a book which would serve as an exact guide to other philanthropically inclined groups who might wish to follow the example of cooperative adoption; but the first day of actual contact with her problem had chilled her. She had put nothing down in her note-book. She had made no scientific progress. There seemed to be no intellectual response in the child.

Peter had set all these things right for her. He had shown her the child's uncompromising integrity of spirit. The keynote of Beulah's nature was, as Jimmie said, that she "had to be shown." Peter pointed out the fact to her that Eleanor's slogan also was, "No compromise." As Eleanor became more familiar with her surroundings this spirit became more and more evident.

"I could let down the hem of these dresses, Aunt Beulah," she said one day, looking down at the long stretch of leg protruding from the chic blue frock that made her look like a Boutet de Monvil. "I can't hem very good, but my stitches don't show much."

"That dress isn't too short, dear. It's the way little girls always wear them. Do little girls on Cape Cod wear them longer?"

"Yes, Aunt Beulah."

"How long do they wear them?"

"Albertina," they had reached the point of discussion of Albertina now, and Beulah was proud of it, "wore her dresses to her ankles, be—because her—her legs was so fat. She said that mine was—were getting to be fat too, and it wasn't refined to wear short dresses, when your legs were fat."

"There are a good many conflicting ideas of refinement in the world, Eleanor," Beulah said.

"I've noticed there are, since I came to New York," Eleanor answered unexpectedly.

Beulah's academic spirit recognized and rejoiced in the fact that with all her docility, Eleanor held firmly to her preconceived notions. She continued to wear her dresses short, but when she was not actually on exhibition, she hid her long legs behind every available bit of furniture or drapery.

The one doubt left in her mind, of the child's initiative and executive ability, was destined to be dissipated by the rather heroic measures sometimes resorted to by a superior agency taking an ironic hand in the game of which we have been too inhumanly sure.

On the fifth week of Eleanor's stay Beulah became a real aunt, the cook left, and her own aunt and official chaperon, little Miss Prentis, was laid low with an attack of inflammatory rheumatism. Beulah's excitement on these various counts, combined with indiscretions in the matter of overshoes and overfatigue, made her an easy victim to a wandering grip germ. She opened her eyes one morning only to shut them with a groan of pain. There was an ache in her head and a thickening in her chest, the significance of which she knew only too well. She found herself unable to rise. She lifted a hoarse voice and called for Mary, the maid, who did not sleep in the house but was due every morning at seven. But the gentle knock on the door was followed by the entrance of Eleanor, not Mary.

"Mary didn't come, Aunt Beulah. I thought you was—were so tired, I'd let you have your sleep out. I heard Miss Prentis calling, and I made her some gruel, and I got my own breakfast."

"Oh! how dreadful," Beulah gasped in the face of this new calamity; "and I'm really so sick. I don't know what we'll do."

Eleanor regarded her gravely. Then she put a professional hand on her pulse and her forehead.

"You've got the grip," she announced.

"I'm afraid I have, Eleanor, and Doctor Martin's out of town, and won't be back till to-morrow when he comes to Aunt Ann. I don't know what we'll do."

"I'll tend to things," Eleanor said. "You lie still and close your eyes, and don't put your arms out of bed and get chilled."

"Well, you'll have to manage somehow," Beulah moaned; "how, I don't know, I'm sure. Give Aunt Annie her medicine and hot water bags, and just let me be. I'm too sick to care what happens."

After the door had closed on the child a dozen things occurred to Beulah that might have been done for her. She was vaguely faint for her breakfast. Her feet were cold. She thought of the soothing warmth of antiphlogistine when applied to the chest. She thought of the quinine on the shelf in the bathroom. Once more she tried lifting her head, but she could not accomplish a sitting posture. She shivered as a draft from the open window struck her.

"If I could only be taken in hand this morning," she thought, "I know it could be broken."

The door opened softly. Eleanor, in the cook's serviceable apron of gingham that would have easily contained another child the same size, swung the door open with one hand and held it to accommodate the passage of the big kitchen tray, deeply laden with a heterogeneous collection of objects. She pulled two chairs close to the bedside and deposited her burden upon them. Then she removed from the tray a goblet of some steaming fluid and offered it to Beulah.

"It's cream of wheat gruel," she said, and added ingratiatingly: "It tastes nice in a tumbler."

Beulah drank the hot decoction gratefully and found, to her surprise, that it was deliciously made.

Eleanor took the glass away from her and placed it on the tray, from which she took what looked to Beulah like a cloth covered omelet,—at any rate, it was a crescent shaped article slightly yellow in tone. Eleanor tested it with a finger.

"It's just about right," she said. Then she fixed Beulah with a stern eye. "Open your chest," she commanded, "and show me the spot where it's worst. I've made a meal poultice."

Beulah hesitated only a second, then she obeyed meekly. She had never seen a meal poultice before, but the heat on her afflicted chest was grateful to her. Antiphlogistine was only Denver mud anyhow. Meekly, also, she took the six grains of quinine and the weak dose of jamaica ginger and water that she was next offered. She felt encouraged and refreshed enough by this treatment to display some slight curiosity when the little girl produced a card of villainous looking safety-pins.

"I'm going to pin you in with these, Aunt Beulah," she said, "and then sweat your cold out of you."

"Indeed, you're not," Beulah said; "don't be absurd, Eleanor. The theory of the grip is—," but she was addressing merely the vanishing hem of cook's voluminous apron.

The child returned almost instantly with three objects of assorted sizes that Beulah could not identify. From the outside they looked like red flannel and from the way Eleanor handled them it was evident that they also were hot.

"I het—heated the flatirons," Eleanor explained, "the way I do for Grandma, and I'm going to spread 'em around you, after you're pinned in the blankets, and you got to lie there till you prespire, and prespire good."

"I won't do it," Beulah moaned, "I won't do any such thing. Go away, child."

"I cured Grandma and Grandpa and Mrs. O'Farrel's aunt that I worked for, and I'm going to cure you," Eleanor said.

"No."

Eleanor advanced on her threateningly.

"Put your arms under those covers," she said, "or I'll dash a glass of cold water in your face,"—and Beulah obeyed her.

Peter nodded wisely when Beulah, cured by these summary though obsolete methods, told the story in full detail. Gertrude had laughed until the invalid had enveloped herself in the last few shreds of her dignity and ordered her out of the room, and the others had been scarcely more sympathetic.

"I know that it's funny, Peter," she said, "but you see, I can't help worrying about it just the same. Of course, as soon as I was up she was just as respectful and obedient to my slightest wish as she ever was, but at the time, when she was lording it over me so, she—she actually slapped me. You never saw such a—blazingly determined little creature."

Peter smiled,—gently, as was Peter's way when any friend of his made an appeal to him.

"That's all right, Beulah," he said, "don't you let it disturb you for an instant. This manifestation had nothing to do with our experiment. Our experiment is working fine—better than I dreamed it would ever work. What happened to Eleanor, you know, was simply this. Some of the conditions of her experience were recreated suddenly, and she reverted."

CHAPTER VI

The entrance into the dining-room of the curly headed young man and his pretty little niece, who had a suite on the eighth floor, as the room clerk informed all inquirers, was always a matter of interest to the residents of the Hotel Winchester. They were an extremely picturesque pair to the eye seeking for romance and color. The child had the pure, clear cut features of the cameo type of New England maidenhood. She was always dressed in some striking combination of blue, deep blue like her eyes, with blue hair ribbons. Her good-looking young relative, with hair almost as near the color of the sun as her own, seemed to be entirely devoted to her, which, considering the charm of the child and the radiant and magnetic spirit of the young man himself, was a delightfully natural manifestation.

But one morning near the close of the second week of their stay, the usual radiation of resilient youth was conspicuously absent from the young man's demeanor, and the child's face reflected the gloom that sat so incongruously on the contour of an optimist. The little girl fumbled her menu card, but the waitress—the usual aging pedagogic type of the small residential hotel—stood unnoticed at the young man's elbow for some minutes before he was sufficiently aroused from his gloomy meditations to address her. When he turned to her at last, however, it was with the grin that she had grown to associate with him,—the grin, the absence of which had kept her waiting behind his chair with a patience that she was, except in a case where her affections were involved, entirely incapable of. Jimmie's protestations of inability to make headway with the ladies were not entirely sincere.

"Bring me everything on the menu," he said, with a wave of his hand in the direction of that painstaking pasteboard. "Coffee, tea, fruit, marmalade, breakfast food, ham and eggs. Bring my niece here the same. That's all." With another wave of the hand he dismissed her.

"You can't eat it all, Uncle Jimmie," Eleanor protested.

"I'll make a bet with you," Jimmie declared. "I'll bet you a dollar to a doughnut that if she brings it all, I'll eat it."

"Oh! Uncle Jimmie, you know she won't bring it. You never bet so I can get the dollar,—you never do."

"I never bet so I can get my doughnut, if it comes to that."

"I don't know where to buy any doughnuts," Eleanor said; "besides, Uncle Jimmie, I don't really consider that I owe them. I never really say that I'm betting, and you tell me I've lost before I've made up my mind anything about it."

"Speaking of doughnuts," Jimmie said, his face still wearing the look of dejection under a grin worn awry, "can you cook, Eleanor? Can you roast a steak, and saute baked beans, and stew sausages, and fry out a breakfast muffin? Does she look like a cook to you?" he suddenly demanded of the waitress, who was serving him, with an apologetic eye on the menu, the invariable toast-coffee-and-three-minute-egg breakfast that he had eaten every morning since his arrival.

The waitress smiled toothily. "She looks like a capable one," she pronounced.

"I *can* cook, Uncle Jimmie," Eleanor giggled, "but not the way you said. You don't roast steak, or—or—"

"Don't you?" Jimmie asked with the expression of pained surprise that never failed to make his ward wriggle with delight. There were links in the educational scheme that Jimmie forged better than any of the cooperative guardians. Not even Jimmie realized the value of the giggle as a developing factor in Eleanor's existence. He took three swallows of coffee and frowned into his cup. "I can make coffee," he added. "Good coffee. Well, we may as well look the facts in the face, Eleanor. The jig's up. We're moving away from this elegant hostelry to-morrow."

"Are we?" Eleanor asked.

"Yes, Kiddo. Apologies to Aunt Beulah (mustn't call you Kiddo) and the reason is, that I'm broke. I haven't got any money at all, Eleanor, and I don't know where I am going to get any. You see, it is this way. I lost my job six weeks ago."

"But you go to work every morning, Uncle Jimmie?"

"I leave the house, that is. I go looking for work, but so far no nice juicy job has come rolling down into my lap. I haven't told you this before because,—well—when Aunt Beulah comes down every day to give you your lessons I wanted it to look all O. K. I thought if you didn't know, you couldn't forget sometime and tell her."

"I don't tattle tale," Eleanor said.

"I know you don't, Eleanor. It's only my doggone pride that makes me want to keep up the bluff, but you're a game kid,—you—know. I tried to get you switched off to one of the others till I could get on my feet, but—no, they just thought I had stage fright. I couldn't insist. It would be pretty humiliating to me to admit that I couldn't support one-sixth of a child that I'd given my solemn oath to be-parent."

"To—to what?"

"Be-parent, if it isn't a word, I invent it. It's awfully tough luck for you, and if you want me to I'll own up to the crowd that I can't swing you, but if you are willing to stick, why, we'll fix up some kind of a way to cut down expenses and bluff it out."

Eleanor considered the prospect. Jimmie watched her apparent hesitation with some dismay.

"Say the word," he declared, "and I'll tell 'em."

"Oh! I don't want you to tell 'em," Eleanor cried. "I was just thinking. If you could get me a place, you know, I could go out to work. You don't eat very much for a man, and I might get my meals thrown in—"

"Don't, Eleanor, don't," Jimmie agonized. "I've got a scheme for us all right. This—this embarrassment is only temporary. The day will come when I can provide you with Pol Roge and diamonds. My father is rich, you know, but he swore to me that I couldn't support myself, and I swore to him that I could, and if I don't do it, I'm damned. I am really, and that isn't swearing."

"I know it isn't, when you mean it the way they say in the Bible."

"I don't want the crowd to know. I don't want Gertrude to know. She hasn't got much idea of me anyway. I'll get another job, if I can only hold out."

"I can go to work in a store," Eleanor cried. "I can be one of those little girls in black dresses that runs between counters."

"Do you want to break your poor Uncle James' heart, Eleanor,—do you?"

"No, Uncle Jimmie."

"Then listen to me. I've borrowed a studio, a large barnlike studio on Washington Square, suitably equipped with pots and pans and kettles. Also, I am going to borrow the wherewithal to keep us going. It isn't a bad kind of place if anybody likes it. There's one dinky little bedroom for you and a cot bed for me, choked in bagdad. If you could kind of engineer the cooking end of it, with me to do the dirty work, of course, I think we could be quite snug and cozy."

"I know we could, Uncle Jimmie," Eleanor said. "Will Uncle Peter come to see us just the same?"

It thus befell that on the fourteenth day of the third month of her residence in New York, Eleanor descended into Bohemia. Having no least suspicion of the real state of affairs—for Jimmie, like most apparently expansive people who are given to rattling nonsense, was actually very reticent about his own business—the other members of the sextette did not hesitate to show their chagrin and disapproval at the change in his manner of living.

"The Winchester was an ideal place for Eleanor," Beulah wailed. "It's deadly respectable and middle class, but it was just the kind of atmosphere for her to accustom herself to. She was learning to manage herself so prettily. This morning when I went to the studio—I wanted to get the lessons over early, and take Eleanor to see that exhibition of Bavarian dolls at Kuhner's—I found her washing up a trail of dishes in that closet behind the screen—you've seen it, Gertrude?—like some poor little scullery maid. She said that Jimmie had made an omelet for breakfast. If he'd made fifty omelets there couldn't have been a greater assortment of dirty dishes and kettles."

Gertrude smiled.

"Jimmie made an omelet for me once for which he used two dozen eggs. He kept breaking them until he found the yolks of a color to suit him. He said pale yolks made poor omelets, so he threw all the pale ones away."

"I suppose that you sat by and let him," Beulah said. "You would let Jimmie do anything. You're as bad as Margaret is about David."

"Or as bad as you are about Peter."

"There we go, just like any silly, brainless girls, whose chief object in life is the—the other sex," Beulah cried inconsistently. "Oh! I hate that kind of thing."

"So do I—in theory—" Gertrude answered, a little dreamily. "Where do Jimmie and Eleanor get the rest of their meals?"

"I can't seem to find out," Beulah said. "I asked Eleanor point-blank this morning what they had to eat last night and where they had it, and she said, 'That's a secret, Aunt Beulah.' When I asked her why it was a secret and who it was a secret with, she only looked worried, and said she guessed she wouldn't talk about it at all because that was the only way to be safe about tattling. You know what I think—I think Jimmie is taking her around to the cafés and all the shady extravagant restaurants. He thinks it's sport and it keeps him from getting bored with the child."

"Well, that's one way of educating the young," Gertrude said, "but I think you are wrong, Beulah."

CHAPTER VII

ONE DESCENT INTO BOHEMIA

"Aunt Beulah does not think that Uncle Jimmie is bringing me up right," Eleanor confided to the pages of her diary. "She comes down here and is very uncomforterble. Well he is bringing me up good, in some ways better than she did. When he swears he always puts out his hand for me to slap him. He had enough to swear of. He can't get any work or earn wages. The advertisement business is on the bum this year becase times are so hard up. The advertisers have to save their money and advertising agents are failing right and left. So poor Uncle Jimmie can't get a place to work at.

"The people in the other studios are very neighborly. Uncle Jimmie leaves a sine on the door when he goes out. It says 'Don't Knock.' They don't they come right in and borrow things. Uncle Jimmie says not to have much to do with them, becase they are so queer, but when I am not at home, the ladies come to call on him, and drink Moxie or something. I know becase once I caught them. Uncle Jimmie says I shall not have Behemiar thrust upon me by him, and to keep away from these ladies until I grow up and then see if I like them. Aunt Beulah thinks that Uncle Jimmie takes me around to other studios and I won't tell but he does not take me anywhere except to walk and have ice-cream soda, but I say I don't want it because of saving the ten cents. We cook on an old gas stove that smells. I can't do very good housekeeping becase things are not convenient. I haven't any oven to do a Saturday baking in, and Uncle Jimmie won't let me do the washing. I should feel more as if I earned my keap if I baked beans and made boiled dinners and layer cake, but in New York they don't eat much but hearty food and saluds. It isn't stylish to have cake and pie and pudding all at one meal. Poor Grandpa would starve. He eats pie for his breakfast, but if I told anybody they would laugh. If I wrote Albertina what folks eat in New York she would laugh.

"Uncle Jimmie is teaching me to like salud. He laughs when I cut up lettice and put sugar on it. He teaches me to like olives and dried up sausages and sour crought. He says it is important to be edjucated in eating, and everytime we go to the Delicate Essenn store to buy something that will edjucate me better. He teaches me to say 'I beg your pardon,' and 'Polly vous Fransay?' and to courtesy and how to enter a room the way you do in private theatricals. He says it isn't knowing these things so much as knowing when you do them that counts, and then Aunt Beulah complains that I am not being brought up.

"I have not seen Uncle Peter for a weak. He said he was going away. I miss him. I would not have to tell him how I was being brought up, and whether I was hitting the white lights as Uncle Jimmie says.—He would know."

Eleanor did not write Albertina during the time when she was living in the studio. Some curious inversion of pride kept her silent on the subject of the change in her life. Albertina would have turned up her nose at the studio, Eleanor knew. Therefore, she would not so much as address an envelope to that young lady from an interior which she would have beheld with scorn. She held long conversations with Gwendolyn, taking the part of Albertina, on the subject of this snobbishness of attitude.

"Lots of people in New York have to live in little teny, weeny rooms, Albertina," she would say. "Rents are perfectly awful here. This studio is so big I get tired dusting all the way round it, and even if it isn't furnished very much, why, think how much furnishing would cost, and carpets and gold frames for the pictures! The pictures that are in here already, without any frames, would sell for hundreds of dollars apiece if the painter could get anybody to buy them. You ought to be very thankful for such a place, Albertina, instead of feeling so stuck up that you pick up your skirts from it."

But Albertina's superiority of mind was impregnable. Her spirit sat in judgment on all the conditions of Eleanor's new environment. She seemed to criticize everything. She hated the nicked, dun colored dishes they ate from, and the black bottomed pots and pans that all the energy of Eleanor's energetic little elbow could not restore to decency again. She hated the cracked, dun colored walls, and the mottled floor that no amount of sweeping and dusting seemed to make an impression on. She hated the compromise of housekeeping in an attic,—she who had been bred in an atmosphere of shining nickle-plated ranges and linoleum, where even the kitchen pump gleamed brightly under its annual coat of good green paint. She hated the compromise, that was the burden of her complaint—either in the person of Albertina or Gwendolyn, whether she lay in the crook of Eleanor's arm in the lumpy bed where she reposed at the end of the day's labor, or whether she sat bolt upright on the lumpy cot in the studio, the broken bisque arm, which Jimmie insisted on her wearing in a sling whenever he was present, dangling limply at her side in the relaxation Eleanor preferred for it.

The fact of not having adequate opportunity to keep her house in order troubled the child, for her days were zealously planned by her enthusiastic guardians. Beulah came at ten o'clock every morning to give her lessons. As Jimmie's quest for work grew into a more and more disheartening adventure, she had difficulty in getting him out of bed in time to prepare and clear away the breakfast for Beulah's arrival. After lunch, to which Jimmie scrupulously came home, she was supposed to work an hour at her modeling clay. Gertrude, who was doing very promising work at the art league, came to the studio twice a week to give her instruction in handling it. Later in the afternoon one of the aunts or uncles usually appeared with some scheme to divert her. Margaret was telling her the stories of the Shakespeare plays, and David was trying to make a card player of her, but was not succeeding as well as if Albertina had not been brought up a hard shell Baptist, who thought card playing a device of the devil's. Peter alone did not come, for even when he was in town he was busy in the afternoon.

As soon as her guests were gone, Eleanor hurried through such housewifely tasks as were possible of accomplishment at that hour, but the strain was telling on her. Jimmie began to realize this and it added to his own distress. One night to save her the labor of preparing the meal, he took her to an Italian restaurant in the neighborhood where the food was honest and palatable, and the service at least deft and clean.

Eleanor enjoyed the experience extremely, until an incident occurred which robbed her evening of its sweetness and plunged her into the purgatory of the child who has inadvertently broken one of its own laws.

Among the belongings in the carpetbag, which was no more—having been supplanted by a smart little suit-case marked with her initials—was a certificate from the Massachusetts Total Abstinence Society, duly signed by herself, and witnessed by the grammar-school teacher and the secretary of the organization. On this certificate (which was decorated by many presentations in dim black and white of mid-Victorian domestic life, and surmounted by a collection of scalloped clouds in which drifted three amateur looking angels amid a crowd of more professional cherubim) Eleanor had pledged herself to abstain from the use as a beverage of all intoxicating drinks, and from the manufacture or traffic in them. She had also subscribed herself as willing to make direct and persevering efforts to extend the principles and blessings of total abstinence.

"Red ink, Andrea," her Uncle Jimmie had demanded, as the black-eyed waiter bent over him, "and ginger ale for the offspring." Eleanor giggled. It was fun to be with Uncle Jimmie in a restaurant again. He always called for something new and unexpected when he spoke of her to the waiter, and he was always what Albertina would consider "very comical" when he talked to him. "But stay," he added holding up an admonitory finger, "I think we'll give the little one *eau rougie* this time. Wouldn't you like *eau rougie*, tinted water, Eleanor, the way the French children drink it?"

Unsuspectingly she sipped the mixture of water and ice and sugar, and "red ink" from the big brown glass bottle that the glowing waiter set before them.

As the meal progressed Jimmie told her that the grated cheese was sawdust and almost made her believe it. He showed her how to eat spaghetti without cutting it and pointed out to her various Italian examples of his object lesson; but she soon realized that in spite of his efforts to entertain her, he was really very unhappy.

"I've borrowed all the money I can, Angelface," he confessed finally. "Tomorrow's the last day of grace. If I don't land that job at the Perkins agency I'll have to give in and tell Peter and David, or wire Dad."

"You could get some other kind of a job," Eleanor said; "plumbing or clerking or something." On Cape Cod the plumber and the grocer's clerk lost no caste because of their calling. "Couldn't you?"

"I *could* so demean myself, and I will. I'll be a chauffeur, I can run a car all right; but the fact remains that by to-morrow something's got to happen, or I've got to own up to the bunch."

Eleanor's heart sank. She tried hard to think of something to comfort him but she could not. Jimmie mixed her more *eau rougie* and she drank it. He poured a full glass, undiluted, for himself, and held it up to the light.

"Well, here's to crime, daughter," he said. "Long may it wave, and us with it."

"That isn't really red ink, is it?" she asked. "It's an awfully pretty color—like grape juice."

"It is grape juice, my child, if we don't inquire too closely into the matter. The Italians are like the French in the guide book, 'fond of dancing and light wines.' This is one of the light wines they are fond of.—Hello, do you feel sick, child? You're white as a ghost. It's the air. As soon as I can get hold of that sacrificed waiter we'll get out of here."

Eleanor's sickness was of the spirit, but at the moment she was incapable of telling him so, incapable of any sort of speech. A great wave of faintness encompassed her. She had broken her pledge. She had lightly encouraged a departure from the blessings and principles of total abstinence.

That night in her bed she made a long and impassioned apology to her Maker for the sin of intemperance into which she had been so unwittingly betrayed. She promised Him that she would never drink anything that came out of a bottle again. She reviewed sorrowfully her many arguments with Albertina— Albertina in the flesh that is—on the subject of bottled drinks in general, and decided that again that virtuous child was right in her condemnation of any drink, however harmless in appearance or nomenclature, that bore the stigma of a bottled label.

She knew, however, that something more than a prayer for forgiveness was required of her. She was pledged to protest against the evil that she had seemingly countenanced. She could not seek the sleep of the innocent until that reparation was made. Through the crack of her sagging door she saw the light from Jimmie's reading lamp and knew that he was still dressed, or clothed at least, with a sufficient regard for the conventionalities to permit her intrusion. She rose and rebraided her hair and tied a daytime ribbon on it. Then she put on her stockings and her blue Japanese kimono—real Japanese, as Aunt Beulah explained, made for a Japanese lady of quality—and made her way into the studio.

Jimmie was not sitting in the one comfortable studio chair with his book under the light and his feet on the bamboo tea table as usual. He was not sitting up at all. He was flung on the couch with his face buried in the cushions, and his shoulders were shaking. Eleanor seeing him thus, forgot her righteous purpose, forgot her pledge to disseminate the principles and blessings of abstinence, forgot everything but the pitiful spectacle of her gallant Uncle Jimmie in grief. She stood looking down at him without quite the courage to kneel at his side to give him comfort.

"Uncle Jimmie," she said, "Uncle Jimmie."

At the sound of her voice he put out his hand to her, gropingly, but he did not uncover his face or shift his position. She found herself smoothing his hair, gingerly at first, but with more and more conviction as he snuggled his boyish head closer.

"I'm awfully discouraged," he said in a weak muffled voice. "I'm sorry you caught me at it, Baby."

Eleanor put her face down close to his as he turned it to her.

"Everything will be all right," she promised him, "everything will be all right. You'll soon get a job—tomorrow maybe."

Then she gathered him close in her angular, tense little arms and held him there tightly. "Everything will be all right," she repeated soothingly; "now you just put your head here, and have your cry out."

CHAPTER VIII

THE TEN HUTCHINSONS

"My Aunt Margaret has a great many people living in her family," Eleanor wrote to Albertina from her new address on Morningside Heights. "She has a mother and a father, and two (2) grandparents, one (1) aunt, one (1) brother, one (1) married lady and the boy of the lady, I think the married lady is a sister but I do not ask any one, oh—and another brother, who does not live here only on Saturdays and Sundays. Aunt Margaret makes ten, and they have a man to wait on the table. His name is a butler. I guess you have read about them in stories. I am taken right in to be one of the family, and I have a good time every day now. Aunt Margaret's father is a college teacher, and Aunt Margaret's grandfather looks like the father of his country. You know who I mean George Washington. They have a piano here that plays itself like a sewing machine. They let me do it. They have after-dinner coffee and gold spoons to it. I guess you would like to see a gold spoon. I did. They are about the size of the tin spoons we had in our playhouse. I have a lot of fun with that boy too. At first I thought he was very affected, but that is just the way they teach him to talk. He is nine and plays tricks on other people. He dares me to do things that I don't do, like go down-stairs and steal sugar. If Aunt Margaret's mother was my grandma I might steal sugar or plum cake. I don't know. Remember the time we took your mother's hermits? I do. I would like to see you. You would think this house was quite a grand house. It has three (3) flights of stairs and one basement. I sleep on the top floor in a dressing room out of Aunt Margaret's only it isn't a dressing room. I dress there but no one else can. Aunt Margaret is pretty and sings lovely. Uncle David comes here a lot. I must close. With love and kisses."

In her diary she recorded some of the more intimate facts of her new existence, such facts as she instinctively guarded from Albertina's calculating sense.

"Everybody makes fun of me here. I don't care if they do, but I can't eat so much at the table when every one is laughing at me. They get me to talking and then they laugh. If I could see anything to laugh at, I would laugh too. They laugh in a refined way but they laugh. They call me Margaret's protegay. They are good to me too. They say to my face that I am like a merry wilkins story and too good to be true, and New England projuces lots of real art, and I am art, I can't remember all the things, but I guess they mean well. Aunt Margaret's grandfather sits at the head of the table, and talks about things I never heard of before. He knows the govoner and does not like the way he parts his hair. I thought all govoners did what they wanted to with their hairs or anything and people had to like it because (I used to spell because wrong but I spell better now) they was the govoners, but it seems not at all.

"Aunt Margaret is lovely to me. We have good times. I meant to like Aunt Beulah the best because she has done the most for me but I am afrayd I don't. I would not cross my heart and say so. Aunt Margaret gives me the lessons now. I guess I learn most as much as I learned I mean was taught of Aunt Beulah. Oh dear sometimes I get descouraged on account of its being such a funny world and so many diferent people in it. And so many diferent feelings. I was afrayd of the hired butler, but I am not now."

―――――――――――――

Eleanor had not made a direct change from the Washington Square studio to the ample house of the Hutchinsons, and it was as well for her that a change in Jimmie's fortunes had taken her back to the Winchester and enabled her to accustom herself again to the amenities of gentler living. Like all sensitive and impressionable children she took on the color of a new environment very quickly. The strain of her studio experience had left her a little cowed and unsure of herself, but she had brightened up like a flower set in the cheerful surroundings of the Winchester and under the influence of Jimmie's restored spirits.

The change had come about on Jimmie's "last day of grace." He had secured the coveted position at the Perkins agency at a slight advance over the salary he had received at the old place. He had left Eleanor in the morning determined to face becomingly the disappointment that was in store for him, and to accept the bitter necessity of admitting his failure to his friends. He had come back in the late afternoon with his fortunes restored, the long weeks of humiliation wiped out, and his life back again on its old confident and inspired footing.

He had burst into the studio with his news before he understood that Eleanor was not alone, and inadvertently shared the secret with Gertrude, who had been waiting for him with the kettle alight and some wonderful cakes from "Henri's" spread out on the tea table. The three had celebrated by dining together at a festive down-town hotel and going back to his studio for coffee. At parting they had solemnly and severally kissed one another. Eleanor lay awake in the dark for a long time that night softly rubbing the cheek that had been so caressed, and rejoicing that the drink Uncle Jimmie had called a high-ball and had pledged their health with so assiduously, had come out of two glasses instead of a bottle.

Her life at the Hutchinsons' was almost like a life on another planet. Margaret was the younger, somewhat delicate daughter of a family of rather strident academics. Professor Hutchinson was not dependent on his salary to defray the expenses of his elegant establishment, but on his father, who had inherited from his father in turn the substantial fortune on which the family was founded.

Margaret was really a child of the fairies, but she was considerably more fortunate in her choice of a foster family than is usually the fate of the foundling. The rigorous altitude of intellect in which she was reared served as a corrective to the oversensitive quality of her imagination.

Eleanor, who in the more leisurely moments of her life was given to visitations from the poetic muse, was inspired to inscribe some lines to her on one of the pink pages of the private diary. They ran as follows, and even Professor Hutchinson, who occupied the chair of English in that urban community of learning that so curiously bisects the neighborhood of Harlem, could not have designated Eleanor's description of his daughter as one that did not describe.

"Aunt Margaret is fair and kind,
And very good and tender.
She has a very active mind.
Her figure is quite slender.

"She moves around the room with grace,
Her hands she puts with quickness.
Although she wears upon her face
The shadow of a sickness."

It was this "shadow of a sickness," that served to segregate Margaret to the extent that was really necessary for her well being. To have shared perpetually in the almost superhuman activities of the family might have forever dulled that delicate spirit to which Eleanor came to owe so much in the various stages of her development.

Margaret put her arm about the child after the ordeal of the first dinner at the big table.

"Father does not bite," she said, "but Grandfather does. The others are quite harmless. If Grandfather shows his teeth, run for your life."

"I don't know where to run to," Eleanor answered seriously, whereupon Margaret hugged her. Her Aunt Margaret would have been puzzling to Eleanor beyond any hope of extrication, but for the quick imagination that unwound her riddles almost as she presented them. For one terrible minute

Eleanor had believed that Hugh Hutchinson senior did bite, he looked so much like some of the worst of the pictures in Little Red Riding Hood.

"While you are here I'm going to pretend you're my very own child," Margaret told Eleanor that first evening, "and we'll never, never tell anybody all the foolish games we play and the things we say to each other. I can just barely manage to be grown up in the bosom of my family, and when I am in the company of your esteemed Aunt Beulah, but up here in my room, Eleanor, I am never grown up. I play with dolls."

"Oh! do you really?"

"I really do," Margaret said. She opened a funny old chest in the corner of the spacious, high studded chamber. "And here are some of the dolls that I play with." She produced a manikin dressed primly after the manner of eighteen-thirty, prim parted hair over a small head festooned with ringlets, a fichu, and mits painted on her fingers. "Beulah," she said with a mischievous flash of a grimace at Eleanor. "Gertrude,"—a dashing young brunette in riding clothes. "Jimmie,"—a curly haired dandy. "David,"—a serious creature with a monocle. "I couldn't find Peter," she said, "but we'll make him some day out of cotton and water colors."

"Oh! can you make dolls?" Eleanor cried in delight, "real dolls with hair and different colored eyes?"

"I can make pretty good ones," Margaret smiled; "manikins like these,—a Frenchwoman taught me."

"Oh; did she? And do you play that the dolls talk to each other as if they was—were the persons?"

"Do I?" Margaret assembled the four manikins into a smart little group. The doll Beulah rose,—on her forefinger. "I can't help feeling," mimicked Margaret in a perfect reproduction of Beulah's earnest contralto, "that we're wasting our lives,—criminally dissipating our forces."

The doll Gertrude put up both hands. "I want to laugh," she cried, "won't everybody please stop talking till I've had my laugh out. Thank you, thank you."

"Why, that's just like Aunt Gertrude," Eleanor said. "Her voice has that kind of a sound like a bell, only more ripply."

"Don't be high-brow," Jimmie's lazy baritone besought with the slight burring of the "r's" that Eleanor found so irresistible. "I'm only a poor hard-working, business man."

The doll David took the floor deliberately. "We intend to devote the rest of our lives," he said, "to the care of our beloved cooperative orphan." On that he made a rather over mannered exit, Margaret planting each foot down deliberately until she flung him back in his box. "That's the kind of a silly your Aunt Margaret is," she continued, "but you mustn't ever tell anybody, Eleanor." She clasped the child again in one of her warm, sudden embraces, and Eleanor squeezing her shyly in return was altogether enraptured with her new existence.

"But there isn't any doll for *you*, Aunt Margaret," she cried.

"Oh! yes, there is, but I wasn't going to show her to you unless you asked, because she's so nice. I saved the prettiest one of all to be myself, not because I believe I'm so beautiful, but—but only because I'd like to be, Eleanor."

"I always pretend I'm a princess," Eleanor admitted.

The Aunt Margaret doll was truly a beautiful creation, a little more like Marie Antoinette than her namesake, but bearing a not inconsiderable resemblance to both, as Margaret pointed out, judicially analyzing her features.

Eleanor played with the rabbit doll only at night after this. In the daytime she looked rather battered and ugly to eyes accustomed to the delicate finish of creatures like the French manikins, but after she was tucked away in her cot in the passion flower dressing-room—all of Margaret's belongings and decorations were a faint, pinky lavender,—her dear daughter Gwendolyn, who impersonated Albertina at increasingly rare intervals as time advanced, lay in the hollow of her arm and received her sacred confidences and ministrations as usual.

"When my two (2) months are up here I think I should be quite sorry," she wrote in the diary, "except that I'm going to Uncle Peter next, and him I would lay me down and dee for, only I never get time enough to see him, and know if he wants me to, when I live with him I shall know. Well life is very exciting all the time now. Aunt Margaret brings me up this way. She tells me that she loves me and that I've got beautiful eyes and hair and am sweet. She tells me that all the time. She says she wants to love me up enough to last because I never had love enough before. I like to be loved. Albertina never loves any one, but on Cape Cod nobody loves anybody—not to say so anyway. If a man is getting married they say he *likes* that girl he is going to marry. In New York they act as different as they eat. The Hutchinsons act different from anybody. They do not know Aunt Margaret has adoptid me. Nobody knows I am adoptid but me and my aunts and uncles. Miss Prentis and Aunt Beulah's mother when she came home and all the bohemiar ladies and all the ten Hutchinsons think I am a little visiting girl from the country. It is nobody's business because I am supported out of allowances and salaries, but it makes me feel queer sometimes. I feel like

"'Where did you come from, baby dear,
Out of the nowhere unto the here?'

Also I made this up out of home sweet home.

"'Pleasures and palaces where e'er I may roam,
Be it ever so humble I wish I had a home.'

"I like having six homes, but I wish everybody knew it. I am nothing to be ashamed of. Speaking of homes I asked Aunt Margaret why my aunts and uncles did not marry each other and make it easier for every one. She said they were not going to get married. That was why they adoptid me. 'Am I the same thing as getting married?' I ast. She said no, I wasn't except that I was a responsibility to keep them unselfish and real. Aunt Beulah doesn't believe in marriage. She thinks its beneth her. Aunt Margaret doesn't think she has the health. Aunt Gertrude has to have a career of sculpture, Uncle David has got to marry some one his mother says to or not at all, and does not like to marry anyway. Uncle Jimmie never saw a happy mariage yet and thinks you have a beter time in single blesedness. Uncle Peter did not sign in the book where they said they would adopt me and not marry. They did not want to ask him because he had some trouble once. I wonder what kind! Well I am going to be married sometime. I want a house to do the housework in and a husband and a backyard full of babies. Perhaps I would rather have a hired butler and gold spoons. I don't know yet. Of course I would like to have time to write poetry. I can sculpture too, but I don't want a career of it because it's so dirty."

Physically Eleanor throve exceedingly during this phase of her existence. The nourishing food and regular living, the sympathy established between herself and Margaret, the régime of physical exercise prescribed by Beulah which she had been obliged guiltily to disregard during the strenuous days of her existence in Washington Square, all contributed to the accentuation of her material well-being. She played with Margaret's nephew, and ran up and down stairs on errands for her mother. She listened to the tales related for her benefit by the old people, and gravely accepted the attentions of the two formidable young men of the family, who entertained her with the pianola and excerpts from classic literature and folk lore.

"The We Are Sevens meet every Saturday afternoon," she wrote—on a yellow page this time—"usually at Aunt Beulah's house. We have tea and lots of fun. I am examined on what I have learned but I don't mind it much.

Physically I am found to be very good by measure and waite. My mind is developing alright. I am very bright on the subject of poetry. They do not know whether David Copperfield had been a wise choice for me, but when I told them the story and talked about it they said I had took it right. I don't tell them about the love part of Aunt Margaret's bringing up. Aunt Beulah says it would make me self conscioush to know that I had such pretty eyes and hair. Aunt Gertrude said 'why not mention my teeth to me, then,' but no one seemed to think so. Aunt Beulah says not to develope my poetry because the theory is to strengthen the weak part of the bridge, and make me do arithmetic. 'Drill on the deficiency,' she says. Well I should think the love part was a deficiency, but Aunt Beulah thinks love is weak and beneath her and any one. Uncle David told me privately that he thought I was having the best that could happen to me right now being with Aunt Margaret. I didn't tell him that the David doll always gets put away in the box with the Aunt Margaret doll and nobody else ever, but I should like to have. He thinks she is the best aunt too."

Some weeks later she wrote to chronicle a painful scene in which she had participated.

"I quarreled with the ten Hutchinsons. I am very sorry. They laughed at me too much for being a little girl and a Cape Codder, but they could if they wanted to, but when they laughed at Aunt Margaret for adopting me and the tears came in her eyes I could not bare it. I did not let the cat out of the bag, but I made it jump out. The Grandfather asked me when I was going back to Cape Cod, and I said I hoped never, and then I said I was going to visit Uncle Peter and Aunt Gertrude and Uncle David next. They said 'Uncle David—do you mean David Bolling?' and I did, so I said 'yes.' Then all the Hutchinsons pitched into Aunt Margaret and kept laughing and saying, 'Who is this mysterious child anyway, and how is it that her guardians intrust her to a crowd of scatter brain youngsters for so long?' and then they said 'Uncle David Bolling—*what* does his mother say?' Then Aunt Margaret got very red in the face and the tears started to come, and I said 'I am not a mysterious child, and my Uncle David is as much my Uncle David as they all are,' and then I said 'My Aunt Margaret has got a perfect right to have me intrusted to her at any time, and not to be laughed at for it,' and I went and stood in front of her and gave her my handkercheve.

"Well I am glad somebody has been told that I am properly adoptid, but I am sorry it is the ten Hutchinsons who know."

CHAPTER IX

Uncle Peter treated her as if she were grown up; that was the wonderful thing about her visit to him,—if there could be one thing about it more wonderful than another. From the moment when he ushered her into his friendly, low ceiled drawing-room with its tiers upon tiers of book shelves, he admitted her on terms of equality to the miraculous order of existence that it was the privilege of her life to share. The pink silk coverlet and the elegance of the silver coated steampipes at Beulah's; the implacable British stuffiness at the Winchester which had had its own stolid charm for the lineal descendant of the Pilgrim fathers; the impressively casual atmosphere over which the "hired butler" presided distributing after-dinner gold spoons, these impressions all dwindled and diminished and took their insignificant place in the background of the romance she was living and breathing in Peter's jewel box of an apartment on Thirtieth Street.

Even to more sophisticated eyes than Eleanor's the place seemed to be a realized ideal of charm and homeliness. It was one of the older fashioned duplex apartments designed in a more aristocratic decade for a more fastidious generation, yet sufficiently adapted to the modern insistence on technical convenience. Peter owed his home to his married sister, who had discovered it and leased it and settled it and suddenly departed for a five years' residence in China with her husband, who was as she so often described him, "a blooming Englishman, and an itinerant banker." Peter's domestic affairs were despatched by a large, motherly Irishwoman, whom Eleanor approved of on sight and later came to respect and adore without reservation.

Peter's home was a home with a place in it for her—a place that it was perfectly evident was better with her than without her. She even slept in the bed that Peter's sister's little girl had occupied, and there were pictures on the walls that had been selected for her.

She had been very glad to make her escape from the Hutchinson household. Her "quarrel" with them had made no difference in their relation to her. To her surprise they treated her with an increase of deference after her outburst, and every member of the family, excepting possibly Hugh Hutchinson senior, was much more carefully polite to her. Margaret explained that the family really didn't mind having their daughter a party to the experiment of cooperative parenthood. It appealed to them as a very interesting try-out of modern educational theory, and their own theories of the independence of the individual modified their criticism of Margaret's secrecy in the matter, which was the only criticism they had to make since Margaret had an income of her own accruing from the estate of the aunt for whom she had been named.

"It is very silly of me to be sensitive about being laughed at," Margaret concluded. "I've lived all my life surrounded by people suffering from an acute sense of humor, but I never, never, never shall get used to being held up to ridicule for things that are not funny to me."

"I shouldn't think you would," Eleanor answered devoutly.

In Peter's house there was no one to laugh at her but Peter, and when Peter laughed she considered it a triumph. It meant that there was something she said that he liked. The welcome she had received as a guest in his house and the wonderful evening that succeeded it were among the epoch making hours in Eleanor's life. It had happened in this wise.

The Hutchinson victoria, for Grandmother Hutchinson still clung to the old-time, stately method of getting about the streets of New York, had left her at Peter's door at six o'clock of a keen, cool May evening. Margaret had not been well enough to come with her, having been prostrated by one of the headaches of which she was a frequent victim.

The low door of ivory white, beautifully carved and paneled, with its mammoth brass knocker, the row of window boxes along the cornice a few feet above it, the very look of the house was an experience and an adventure to her. When she rang, the door opened almost instantly revealing Peter on the threshold with his arms open. He had led her up two short flights of stairs—ivory white with carved banisters, she noticed, all as immaculately shining with soap and water as a Cape Cod interior—to his own gracious drawing-room where Mrs. Finnigan was bowing and smiling a warmhearted Irish welcome to her. It was like a wonderful story in a book and her eyes were shining with joy as Uncle Peter pulled out her chair and she sat down to the first meal in her honor. The grown up box of candy at her plate, the grave air with which Peter consulted her tastes and her preferences were all a part of a beautiful magic that had never quite touched her before.

She had been like a little girl in a dream passing dutifully or delightedly through the required phases of her experience, never quite believing in its permanence or reality; but her life with Uncle Peter was going to be real, and her own. That was what she felt the moment she stepped over his threshold.

After their coffee before the open fire—she herself had had "cambric" coffee—Peter smoked his cigar, while she curled up in silence in the twin to his big cushioned chair and sampled her chocolates. The blue flames skimmed the bed of black coals, and finally settled steadily at work on them nibbling and sputtering until the whole grate was like a basket full of molten light, glowing and golden as the hot sun when it sinks into the sea. 106

Except to offer her the ring about his slender Panatela, and to ask her if she were happy, Peter did not speak until he had deliberately crushed out the last spark from his stub and thrown it into the fire. The ceremony over, he held out his arms to her and she slipped into them as if that moment were the one she had been waiting for ever since the white morning looked into the window of the lavender dressing-room on Morningside Heights, and found her awake and quite cold with the excitement of thinking of what the day was to bring forth.

"Eleanor," Peter said, when he was sure she was comfortably arranged with her head on his shoulder, "Eleanor, I want you to feel at home while you are here, really at home, as if you hadn't any other home, and you and I belonged to each other. I'm almost too young to be your father, but—"

"Oh! are you?" Eleanor asked fervently, as he paused.

"—But I can come pretty near feeling like a father to you if it's a father you want. I lost my own father when I was a little older than you are now, but I had my dear mother and sister left, and so I don't know what it's like to be all alone in the world, and I can't always understand exactly how you feel, but you must always remember that I want to understand and that I will understand if you tell me. Will you remember that, Eleanor?"

"Yes, Uncle Peter," she said soberly; then perhaps for the first time since her babyhood she volunteered a caress that was not purely maternal in its nature. She put up a shy hand to the cheek so close to her own and patted it earnestly. "Of course I've got my grandfather and grandmother," she argued, "but they're very old, and not very affectionate, either. Then I have all these new aunts and uncles pretending," she was penetrating to the core of the matter, Peter realized, "that they're just as good as parents. Of course, they're just as good as they can be and they take so much trouble that it mortifies me, but it isn't just the same thing, Uncle Peter!"

"I know," Peter said, "I know, dear, but you must remember we mean well."

"I don't mean you; it isn't you that I think of when I think about my co— co-woperative parents, and it isn't any of them specially,—it's just the idea of—of visiting around, and being laughed at, and not really belonging to anybody."

Peter's arms tightened about her.

"Oh! but you do belong, you do belong. You belong to me, Eleanor."

"That was what I hoped you would say, Uncle Peter," she whispered.

They had a long talk after this, discussing the past and the future; the past few months of the experiment from Eleanor's point of view, and the future in relation to its failures and successes. Beulah was to begin giving her lessons again and she was to take up music with a visiting teacher on Peter's piano. (Eleanor had not known it was a piano at first, as she had never seen a baby grand before. Peter did not know what a triumph it was when she made herself put the question to him.)

"If my Aunt Beulah could teach me as much as she does and make it as interesting as Aunt Margaret does, I think I would make her feel very proud of me," Eleanor said. "I get so nervous saving energy the way Aunt Beulah says for me to that I forget all the lesson. Aunt Margaret tells too many stories, I guess, but I like them."

"Your Aunt Margaret is a child of God," Peter said devoutly, "in spite of her raw-boned, intellectual family."

"Uncle David says she's a daughter of the fairies."

"She's that, too. When Margaret's a year or two older you won't feel the need of a mother."

"I don't now," said Eleanor; "only a father,—that I want you to be, the way you promised."

"That's done," Peter said. Then he continued musingly, "You'll find Gertrude—different. I can't quite imagine her presiding over your moral welfare but I think she'll be good at it. She's a good deal of a person, you know."

"Aunt Beulah's a good kind of person, too," Eleanor said; "she tries hard. The only thing is that she keeps trying to make me express myself, and I don't know what that means."

"Let me see if I can tell you," said Peter. "Self-expression is a part of every man's duty. Inside we are all trying to be good and true and fine—"

"Except the villains," Eleanor interposed. "People like Iago aren't trying."

"Well, we'll make an exception of the villains; we're talking of people like us, pretty good people with the right instincts. Well then, if all the time we're trying to be good and true and fine, we carry about a blank face that reflects nothing of what we are feeling and thinking, the world is a little worse off, a little duller and heavier place for what is going on inside of us."

"Well, how can we make it better off then?" Eleanor inquired practically.

"By not thinking too much about it for one thing, except to remember to smile, by trying to be just as much at home in it as possible, by letting the kind of person we are trying to be show through on the outside. By gosh! I wish Beulah could hear me."

"By just not being bashful, do you mean?"

"That's the idea."

"Well, when Aunt Beulah makes me do those dancing exercises, standing up in the middle of the floor and telling me to be a flower and express myself as a flower, does she just mean not to be bashful?"

"Something like that: she means stop thinking of yourself and go ahead—"

"But how can I go ahead with her sitting there watching?"

"I suppose I ought to tell you to imagine that you had the soul of a flower, but I haven't the nerve."

"You've got nerve enough to do anything," Eleanor assured him, but she meant it admiringly, and seriously.

"I haven't the nerve to go on with a moral conversation in which you are getting the better of me at every turn," Peter laughed. "I'm sure it's unintentional, but you make me feel like a good deal of an ass, Eleanor."

"That means a donkey, doesn't it?"

"It does, and by jove, I believe that you're glad of it."

"I do rather like it," said Eleanor; "of course you don't really feel like a donkey to me. I mean I don't make you feel like one, but it's funny just pretending that you mean it."

"Oh! woman, woman," Peter cried. "Beulah tried to convey something of the fact that you always got the better of every one in your modest unassuming way, but I never quite believed it before. At any rate it's bedtime, and here comes Mrs. Finnigan to put you to bed. Kiss me good night, sweetheart."

Eleanor flung her arms about his neck, in her first moment of abandonment to actual emotional self-expression if Peter had only known it.

"I will never really get the better of you in my life, Uncle Peter," she promised him passionately.

CHAPTER X

THE OMNISCIENT FOCUS

One of the traditional prerogatives of an Omnipotent Power is to look down at the activities of earth at any given moment and ascertain simultaneously the occupation of any number of people. Thus the Arch Creator—that Being of the Supreme Artistic Consciousness—is able to peer into segregated interiors at His own discretion and watch the plot thicken and the drama develop. Eleanor, who often visualized this proceeding, always imagined a huge finger projecting into space, cautiously tilting the roofs of the Houses of Man to allow the sweep of the Invisible Glance.

Granting the hypothesis of the Divine privilege, and assuming for the purposes of this narrative the Omniscient focus on the characters most concerned in it, let us for the time being look over the shoulder of God and inform ourselves of their various occupations and preoccupations of a Saturday afternoon in late June during the hour before dinner.

Eleanor, in her little white chamber on Thirtieth Street, was engaged in making a pink and green toothbrush case for a going-away gift for her Uncle Peter. To be sure she was going away with him when he started for the Long Island beach hotel from which he proposed to return every day to his office in the city, but she felt that a slight token of her affection would be fitting and proper on the eve of their joint departure. She was hurrying to get it done that she might steal softly into the dining-room and put it on his plate undetected. Her eyes were very wide, her brow intent and serious, and her delicate lips lightly parted. At that moment she bore a striking resemblance to the Botticelli head in Beulah's drawing-room that she had so greatly admired.

Of all the people concerned in her history, she was the most tranquilly occupied.

Peter in the room beyond was packing his trunk and his suit-case. At this precise stage of his proceedings he was trying to make two decisions, equally difficult, but concerned with widely different departments of his consciousness. He was gravely considering whether or not to include among his effects the photograph before him on the dressing-table—that of the girl to whom he had been engaged from the time he was a Princeton sophomore until her death four years later—and also whether or not it would be worth his while to order a new suit of white flannels so late in the season. The fact that he finally decided against the photograph and in favor of the white flannels has nothing to do with the relative importance of the two matters thus engrossing him. The health of the human mind depends largely on its ability to assemble its irrelevant and incongruous problems in dignified yet informal proximity. When he went to his desk it was with the double intention of addressing a letter to his tailor, and locking the cherished photograph in a drawer; but, the letter finished, he still held the picture in his hand and gazed down at it mutely and when the discreet knock on his door that constituted the announcing of dinner came, he was still sitting motionless with the photograph propped up before him.

Up-town, Beulah, whose dinner hour came late, was rather more actively, though possibly not more significantly, occupied. She was doing her best to evade the wild onslaught of a young man in glasses who had been wanting to marry her for a considerable period, and had now broken all bounds in a cumulative attempt to inform her of the fact.

Though he was assuredly in no condition to listen to reason, Beulah was reasoning with him, kindly and philosophically, paying earnest attention to the style and structure of her remarks as she did so. Her emotions, as is usual on such occasions, were decidedly mixed. She was conscious of a very real dismay at her unresponsiveness, a distress for the acute pain from which the distraught young man seemed to be suffering, and the thrill, which had she only known it, is the unfailing accompaniment to the first eligible proposal of marriage. In the back of her brain there was also, so strangely is the human mind constituted, a kind of relief at being able to use mature logic once more, instead of the dilute form of moral dissertation with which she tried to adapt herself to Eleanor's understanding.

"I never intend to marry any one," she was explaining gently. "I not only never intend to, but I am pledged in a way that I consider irrevocably binding never to marry,"—and that was the text from which all the rest of her discourse developed.

Jimmie, equally bound by the oath of celibacy, but not equally constrained by it apparently, was at the very moment when Beulah was so successfully repulsing the familiarity of the high cheek-boned young man in the black and white striped tie, occupied in encouraging a familiarity of a like nature. That is, he was holding the hand of a young woman in the darkened corner of a drawing-room which had been entirely unfamiliar to him ten days before, and was about to impress a caress on lips that seemed to be ready to meet his with a certain degree of accustomed responsiveness. That this was not a peculiarly significant incident in Jimmie's career might have been difficult to explain, at least to the feminine portion of the group of friends he cared most for.

Margaret, dressed for an academic dinner party, in white net with a girdle of pale pink and lavender ribbons, had flung herself face downward on her bed in reckless disregard of her finery; and because it was hot and she was homesick for green fields and the cool stretches of dim wooded country, had transported herself in fancy and still in her recumbent attitude to the floor of a canoe that was drifting down-stream between lush banks of meadow grass studded with marsh lilies. After some interval—and shift of position—the way was arched overhead with whispering trees, the stars came out one by one, showing faintly between waving branches; and she perceived dimly that a figure that was vaguely compounded of David and Peter and the handsomest of all the young kings of Spain, had quietly taken its place in the bow and had busied itself with the paddles,—whereupon she was summoned to dinner, where the ten Hutchinsons and their guests were awaiting her.

David, the only member of the group whose summer vacation had actually begun, was sitting on the broad veranda of an exclusive country club several hundreds of miles away from New York and looking soberly into the eyes of a blue ribbon bull dog, whose heavy jowl rested on his knees. His mother, in one of the most fashionable versions of the season's foulards, sleekly corseted and coifed, was sitting less than a hundred yards away from him, fanning herself with three inches of hand woven fan and contemplating David. In the dressing-room above, just alighted from a limousine de luxe, was a raven-haired, crafty-eyed ingénue (whose presence David did not suspect or he would have recollected a sudden pressing engagement out of her vicinity), preening herself for conquest. David's mind, unlike the minds of the "other gifted members of the We Are Seven Club," to quote Jimmie's most frequent way of referring to them, was to all intents and purposes a total blank. He answered monosyllabically his mother's questions, patted the dog's beetling forehead and thought of nothing at all for practically forty-five minutes. Then he rose, and offering his arm to his mother led her gravely to the table reserved for him in the dining-room.

Gertrude, in her studio at the top of the house in Fifty-sixth Street where she lived with her parents, was putting the finishing touches on a faun's head; and a little because she had unconsciously used Jimmie's head for her model, and a little because of her conscious realization at this moment that the roughly indicated curls over the brow were like nobody's in the world but Jimmie's, she was thinking of him seriously. She was thinking also of the dinner on a tray that would presently be brought up to her, since her mother and father were out of town, and of her coming two months with Eleanor and her recent inspiration concerning them.

In Colhassett, Cape Cod, Massachusetts, the dinner hour and even the supper hour were long past. In the commodious kitchen of Eleanor's former home two old people were sitting in calico valanced rockers, one by either window. The house was a pleasant old colonial structure, now badly run down but still marked with that distinction that only the instincts of aristocracy can bestow upon a decaying habitation.

A fattish child made her way up the walk, toeing out unnecessarily, and let herself in by the back door without knocking.

"Hello, Mis' Chase and Mr. Amos," she said, seating herself in a straight backed, yellow chair, and swinging her crossed foot nonchalantly, "I thought I would come in to inquire about Eleanor. Ma said that she heard that she was coming home to live again. Is she, Mr. Amos?"

Albertina was not a peculiar favorite of Eleanor's grandfather. Amos Chase had ideas of his own about the proper bringing up of children, and the respect due from them to their elders. Also Albertina's father had come from "poor stock." There was a strain of bad blood in her. The women of the Weston families hadn't always "behaved themselves." He therefore answered this representative of the youngest generation rather shortly.

"I don't know nothing about it," he said.

"Why, father," the querulous old voice of Grandmother Chase protested, "you know she's comin' home somewhere 'bout the end of July, she and one of her new aunties and a hired girl they're bringing along to do the work. I don't see why you can't answer the child's question."

"I don't know as I'm obligated to answer any questions that anybody sees fit to put to me."

"Well, I *be*. Albertina, pass me my glasses from off the mantel-tree-shelf, and that letter sticking out from behind the clock and I'll read what she says."

Albertina, with a reproachful look at Mr. Amos, who retired coughing exasperatedly behind a paper that he did not read, allowed herself to be informed through the medium of a letter from Gertrude and a postscript from Eleanor of the projected invasion of the Chase household.

"I should think you'd rather have Eleanor come home by herself than bringing a strange woman and a hired girl," Albertina contributed a trifle tartly. The distinction of a hired girl in the family was one which she had long craved on her own account.

"All nonsense, I call it," the old man ejaculated.

"Well, Eleena, she writes that she can't get away without one of 'em comin' along with her and I guess we can manage someways. I dunno what work city help will make in this kitchen. You can't expect much from city help. They ain't clean like home folks. I shall certainly be dretful pleased to see Eleena, and so will her grandpa—in spite o' the way he goes on about it."

A snort came from the region of the newspaper.

"I shouldn't think you'd feel as if you had a grandchild now that six rich people has adopted her," Albertina suggested helpfully.

"It's a good thing for the child," her grandmother said. "I'm so lame I couldn't do my duty by her. Old folks is old folks, and they can't do for others like young ones. I'd d'ruther have had her adopted by one father and mother instead o' this passel o' young folks passing her around among themselves, but you can't have what you'd d'ruther have in this world. You got to take what comes and be thankful."

"Did she write you about having gold coffee spoons at her last place?" Albertina asked. "I think they was probably gilded over like ice-cream spoons, and she didn't know the difference. I guess she has got a lot of new clothes. Well, I'll have to be getting along. I'll come in again."

At the precise moment that the door closed behind Albertina, the clock in Peter Stuyvesant's apartment in New York struck seven and Eleanor, in a fresh white dress and blue ribbons, slipped into her chair at the dinner table and waited with eyes blazing with excitement for Peter to make the momentous discovery of the gift at his plate.

CHAPTER XI

"Dear Uncle Peter," Eleanor wrote from Colhassett when she had been established there under the new régime for a week or more. "I slapped Albertina's face. I am very awfully sorry, but I could not help it. Don't tell Aunt Margaret because it is so contrary to her teachings and also the golden rule, but she was more contrary to the golden rule that I was. I mean Albertina. What do you think she said? She said Aunt Gertrude was homely and an old maid, and the hired girl was homely too. Well, I think she is, but I am not going to have Albertina think so. Aunt Gertrude is pretty with those big eyes and ink like hair and lovely teeth and one dimple. Albertina likes hair fuzzed all over faces and blonds. Then she said she guessed I wasn't your favorite, and that the gold spoons were most likely tin gilded over. I don't know what you think about slapping. Will you please write and say what you think? You know I am anxsuch to do well. But I think I know as much as Albertina about some things. She uster treat me like a dog, but it is most a year now since I saw her before.

"Well, here we are, Aunt Gertrude and me, too. Grandpa did not like her at first. She looked so much like summer folks, and acted that way, too. He does not agree with summer folks, but she got him talking about foreign parts and that Spanish girl that made eyes at him, and nearly got him away from Grandma, and the time they were wrecked going around the horn, and showing her dishes and carvings from China. Now he likes her first rate. She laughs all the time. Grandma likes her too, but not when Grandpa tells her about that girl in Spain.

"We eat in the dining-room, and have lovely food, only Grandpa does not like it, but we have him a pie now for breakfast,—his own pie that he can eat from all the time and he feels better. Aunt Gertrude is happy seeing him eat it for breakfast and claps her hands when he does it, only he doesn't see her.

"She is teaching me more manners, and to swim, and some French. It is vacation and I don't have regular lessons, the way I did while we were on Long Island.

"Didn't we have a good time in that hotel? Do you remember the night I stayed up till ten o'clock and we sat on the beach and talked? I do. I love you very much. I think it is nice to love anybody. Only I miss you. I would miss you more if I believed what Albertina said about my not being your favorite. I am.

"I wish you could come down here. Uncle Jimmie is coming and then I don't know what Albertina will say.

"About teaching me. Aunt Gertrude's idea of getting me cultivated is to read to me from the great Masters of literature and funny books too, like Mark Twain and the Nonsense Thology. Then I say what I think of them, and she just lets me develop along those lines, which is pretty good for summer.

"Here is a poem I wrote. I love you best.

"The sun and wind are on the sea,
The waves are clear and blue,
This is the place I like to be,
If I could just have you.

"The insects chirrup in the grass,
The birds sing in the tree,
And oh! how quick the time would pass
If you were here with me."

"What do you think of slapping, Aunt Gertrude?" Eleanor asked one evening when they were walking along the hard beach that the receding tide had left cool and firm for their pathway, and the early moon had illumined for them. "Do you think it's awfully bad to slap any one?"

"I wouldn't slap you, if that's what you mean, Eleanor."

"Would you slap somebody your own size and a little bigger?"

"I might under extreme provocation."

"I thought perhaps you would," Eleanor sighed with a gasp of relieved satisfaction.

"I don't believe in moral suasion entirely, Eleanor," Gertrude tried to follow Eleanor's leads, until she had in some way satisfied the child's need for enlightenment on the subject under discussion. It was not always simple to discover just what Eleanor wanted to know, but Gertrude had come to believe that there was always some excellent reason for her wanting to know it. "I think there are some quarrels that have to be settled by physical violence."

Eleanor nodded. Then,

"What about refinement?" she asked unexpectedly. "I want to bring myself up good when—when all of my aunts and uncles are too busy, or don't know. I want to grow up, and be ladylike and a credit, and I'm getting such good culture that I think I ought to, but—I get worried about my refinement. City refinement is different from country refinement."

"Refinement isn't a thing that you can worry about," Gertrude began slowly. She realized perhaps better than any of the others, being a better balanced, healthier creature than either Beulah or Margaret, that there were serious defects in the scheme of cooperative parentage. Eleanor, thanks to the overconscientious digging about her roots, was acquiring a New England self-consciousness about her processes. A child, Gertrude felt, should be handed a code ready made and should be guided by it without question until his maturer experience led him to modify it. The trouble with trying to explain this to Eleanor was that she had already had too many things explained to her, and the doctrine of unselfconsciousness can not be inculcated by an exploitation of it. "If you are naturally a fine person your instinct will be to do the fine thing. You must follow it when you feel the instinct and not think about it between times."

"That's Uncle Peter's idea," Eleanor said, "that not thinking. Well, I'll try— but you and Uncle Peter didn't have six different parents and a Grandpa and Grandma and Albertina all criticizing your refinement in different ways. Don't you ever have any trouble with your behavior, Aunt Gertrude?"

Gertrude laughed. The truth was that she was having considerable trouble with her behavior since Jimmie's arrival two days before. She had thought to spend her two months with Eleanor on Cape Cod helping the child to relate her new environment to her old, while she had the benefit of her native air and the freedom of a rural summer. She also felt that one of their number ought to have a working knowledge of Eleanor's early surroundings and habits. She had meant to put herself and her own concerns entirely aside. If she had a thought for any one but Eleanor she meant it to be for the two old people whose guest she had constituted herself. She explained all this to Jimmie a day or two before her departure, and to her surprise he had suggested that he spend his own two vacation weeks watching the progress of her experiment. Before she was quite sure of the wisdom of allowing him to do so she had given him permission to come. Jimmie was part of her trouble. Her craving for isolation and undiscovered country; her eagerness to escape with her charge to some spot where she would not be subjected to any sort of familiar surveillance, were all a part of an instinct to segregate herself long enough to work out the problem of Jimmie and decide what to do about it. This she realized as soon as he arrived on the spot. She realized further that she had made practically no progress in the matter, for this curly headed young man, bearing no relation to anything that Gertrude had decided a young man should be, was rapidly becoming a serious menace to her peace of mind, and her ideal of a future lived for art alone. She had definitely begun to realize this on the night when Jimmie, in his exuberance at securing his new job, had seized her about the waist and kissed her on the lips. She had thought a good deal about that kiss, which came dangerously near being her first one. She was too clever, too cool and aloof, to have had many tentative love-affairs. Later, as she softened and warmed and gathered grace with the years she was likely to seem more alluring and approachable to the gregarious male. Now she answered her small interlocutor truthfully.

"Yes, Eleanor, I do have a whole lot of trouble with my behavior. I'm having trouble with it today, and this evening," she glanced up at the moon, which was seemingly throwing out conscious waves of effulgence, "I expect to have more," she confessed.

"Oh! do you?" asked Eleanor, "I'm sorry I can't sit up with you then and help you. You—you don't expect to be—provocated to *slap* anybody, do you?"

"No, I don't, but as things are going I almost wish I did," Gertrude answered, not realizing that before the evening was over there would be one person whom she would be ruefully willing to slap several times over.

As they turned into the village street from the beach road they met Jimmie, who had been having his after-dinner pipe with Grandfather Amos, with whom he had become a prime favorite. With him was Albertina, toeing out more than ever and conversing more than blandly.

"This virtuous child has been urging me to come after Eleanor and remind her that it is bedtime," Jimmie said, indicating the pink gingham clad figure at his side. "She argues that Eleanor is some six months younger than she and ought to be in bed first, and personally she has got to go in the next fifteen minutes."

"It's pretty hot weather to go to bed in," Albertina said. "Miss Sturgis, if I can get my mother to let me stay up half an hour more, will you let Eleanor stay up?"

Just beyond her friend, in the shadow of her ample back, Eleanor was making gestures intended to convey the fact that sitting up any longer was abhorrent to her.

"Eleanor needs her sleep to-night, I think," Gertrude answered, professionally maternal.

"I brought Albertina so that our child might go home under convoy, while you and I were walking on the beach," Jimmie suggested.

As the two little girls fell into step, the beginning of their conversation drifted back to the other two, who stood watching them for a moment.

"I thought I'd come over to see if you was willing to say you were sorry," Albertina began. "My face stayed red in one spot for two hours that day after you slapped me."

"I'm not sorry," Eleanor said ungraciously, "but I'll say that I am, if you've come to make up."

"Well, we won't say any more about it then," Albertina conceded. "Are Miss Sturgis and Mr. Sears going together, or are they just friends?"

"Isn't that Albertina one the limit?" Jimmie inquired, with a piloting hand under Gertrude's elbow. "She told me that she and Eleanor were mad, but she didn't want to stay mad because there was more going on over here than there was at her house and she liked to come over."

"I'm glad Eleanor slapped her," Gertrude said; "still I'm sorry our little girl has uncovered the clay feet of her idol. She's through with Albertina for good."

"Do you know, Gertrude," Jimmy said, as they set foot on the glimmering beach, "you don't seem a bit natural lately. You used to be so full of the everlasting mischief. Every time you opened your mouth I dodged for fear of being spiked. Yet here you are just as docile as other folks."

"Don't you like me—as well?" Gertrude tried her best to make her voice sound as usual.

"Better," Jimmie swore promptly; then he added a qualifying—"I guess."

"Don't you know?" But she didn't allow him the opportunity to answer. "I'm in a transition period, Jimmie," she said. "I meant to be such a good parent to Eleanor and correct all the evil ways into which she has fallen as a result of all her other injudicious training, and, instead of that, I'm doing nothing but think of myself and my own hankerings and yearnings and such. I thought I could do so much for the child."

"That's the way we all think till we tackle her and then we find it quite otherwise and even more so. Tell me about your hankerings and yearnings."

"Tell me about your job, Jimmie."

And for a little while they found themselves on safe and familiar ground again. Jimmie's new position was a very satisfactory one. He found himself associated with men of solidity and discernment, and for the first time in his business career he felt himself appreciated and stimulated by that appreciation to do his not inconsiderable best. Gertrude was the one woman—Eleanor had not yet attained the inches for that classification—to whom he ever talked business.

"Now, at last, I feel that I've got my feet on the earth, Gertrude; as if the stuff that was in me had a chance to show itself, and you don't know what a good feeling that is after you've been marked trash by your family and thrown into the dust heap."

"I'm awfully glad, Jimmie."

"I know you are, 'Trude. You're an awfully good pal. It isn't everybody I'd talk to like this. Let's sit down."

The moonlight beat down upon them in floods of sentient palpitating glory. Little breathy waves sought the shore and whispered to it. The pines on the breast of the bank stirred softly and tenderly.

"Lord, what a night," Jimmie said, and began burying her little white hand in the beach sand. His breath was not coming quite evenly. "Now tell me about your job," he said.

"I don't think I want to talk about my job tonight."

"What do you want to talk about?"

"I don't know." There was no question about her voice sounding as usual this time.

Jimmie brushed the sand slowly away from the buried hand and covered it with his own. He drew nearer, his face close, and closer to hers. Gertrude closed her eyes. It was coming, it was coming and she was glad. That silly old vow of celibacy, her silly old thoughts about art. What was art? What was anything with the arms of the man you loved closing about you. His lips were on hers.

Jimmie drew a sharp breath, and let her go.

"Gertrude," he said, "I'm incorrigible. I ought to be spanked. I'd make love to—Eleanor's grandmother if I had her down here on a night like this. Will you forgive me?"

Gertrude got to her feet a little unsteadily, but she managed a smile.

"It's only the moon," she said, "and—and young blood. I think Grandfather Amos would probably affect me the same way."

Jimmie's momentary expression of blankness passed and Gertrude did not press her advantage. They walked home in silence.

"It's awfully companionable to realize that you also are human, 'Trude," he hazarded on the doorstep.

Gertrude put a still hand into his, which is a way of saying "Good night," that may be more formal than any other.

"The Colonel's lady, and July O'Grady," she quoted lightly. "Good night, Jimmie."

Up-stairs in her great chamber under the eaves, Eleanor was composing a poem which she copied carefully on a light blue page of her private diary. It read as follows:

"To love, it is the saddest thing,
When friendship proves unfit,
For lots of sadness it will bring,
When e'er you think of it.

Alas! that friends should prove untrue
And disappoint you so.
Because you don't know what to do,
And hardly where to go."

———————————————

CHAPTER XII

MADAM BOLLING

"Is this the child, David?"

"Yes, mother."

Eleanor stared impassively into the lenses of Mrs. Bolling's lorgnette.

"This is my mother, Eleanor."

Eleanor courtesied as her Uncle Jimmie had taught her, but she did not take her eyes from Mrs. Bolling's face.

"Not a bad-looking child. I hate this American fashion of dressing children like French dolls, in bright colors and smart lines. The English are so much more sensible. An English country child would have cheeks as red as apples. How old are you?"

"Eleven years old my next birthday."

"I should have thought her younger, David. Have her call me madam. It sounds better."

"Very well, mother. I'll teach her the ropes when the strangeness begins to wear off. This kind of thing is all new to her, you know."

"She looks it. Give her the blue chamber and tell Mademoiselle to take charge of her. You say you want her to have lessons for so many hours a day. Has she brains?"

"She's quite clever. She writes verses, she models pretty well, Gertrude says. It's too soon to expect any special aptitude to develop."

"Well, I'm glad to discover your philanthropic tendencies, David. I never knew you had any before, but this seems to me a very doubtful undertaking. You take a child like this from very plain surroundings and give her a year or two of life among cultivated and well-to-do people, just enough for her to acquire a taste for extravagant living and associations. Then what becomes of her? You get tired of your bargain. Something else comes on the docket. You marry—and then what becomes of your protégée? She goes back to the country, a thoroughly unsatisfied little rustic, quite unfitted to be the wife of the farmer for whom fate intended her."

"I wish you wouldn't, mother," David said, with an uneasy glance at Eleanor's pale face, set in the stoic lines he remembered so well from the afternoon of his first impression of her. "She's a sensitive little creature."

"Nonsense. It never hurts anybody to have a plain understanding of his position in the world. I don't know what foolishness you romantic young people may have filled her head with. It's just as well she should hear common sense from me and I intend that she shall."

"I've explained to you, mother, that this child is my legal and moral responsibility and will be partly at least under my care until she becomes of age. I want her to be treated as you'd treat a child of mine if I had one. If you don't, I can't have her visit us again. I shall take her away with me somewhere. Bringing her home to you this time is only an experiment."

"She'll have a much more healthful and normal experience with us than she's had with any of the rest of your violent young set, I'll be bound. She'll probably be useful, too. She can look out for Zaidee—I never say that name without irritation—but it's the only name the little beast will answer to. Do you like dogs, child?"

Eleanor started at the suddenness of the question, but did not reply to it. Mrs. Bolling waited and David looked at her expectantly.

"My mother asked you if you liked dogs, Eleanor; didn't you understand?"

Eleanor opened her lips as if to speak and then shut them again firmly.

"Your protégée is slightly deaf, David," his mother assured him.

"You can tell her 'yes,'" Eleanor said unexpectedly to David. "I like dogs, if they ain't treacherous."

"She asked you the question," David said gravely; "this is her house, you know. It is she who deserves consideration in it."

"Why can't I talk to you about her, the way she does about me?" Eleanor demanded. "She can have consideration if she wants it, but she doesn't think I'm any account. Let her ask you what she wants and I'll tell you."

"Eleanor," David remonstrated, "Eleanor, you never behaved like this before. I don't know what's got into her, mother."

"She merely hasn't any manners. Why should she have?"

Eleanor fixed her big blue eyes on the lorgnette again.

"If it's manners to talk the way you do to your own children and strange little girls, why, then I don't want any," she said. "I guess I'll be going," she added abruptly and turned toward the door.

David took her by the shoulders and brought her right about face.

"Say good-by to mother," he said sternly.

"Good-by, ma'am—madam," Eleanor said and courtesied primly.

"Tell Mademoiselle to teach her a few things before the next audience, David, and come back to me in fifteen minutes. I have something important to talk over with you."

David stood by the open door of the blue chamber half an hour later and watched Eleanor on her knees, repacking her suit-case. Her face was set in pale determined lines, and she looked older and a little sick. Outside it was blowing a September gale, and the trees were waving desperate branches in the wind. David had thought that the estate on the Hudson would appeal to the little girl. It had always appealed to him so much, even though his mother's habits of migration with the others of her flock at the different seasons had left him so comparatively few associations with it. He had thought she would like the broad sweeping lawns and the cherubim fountain, the apple orchard and the kitchen garden, and the funny old bronze dog at the end of the box hedge. When he saw how she was occupied, he understood that it was not her intention to stay and explore these things.

"Eleanor," he said, stepping into the room suddenly, "what are you doing with your suit-case? Didn't Mademoiselle unpack it for you?" He was close enough now to see the signs of tears she had shed.

"Yes, Uncle David."

"Why are you packing it again?"

Her eyes fell and she tried desperately to control a quivering lip.

"Because I am—I want to go back."

"Back where?"

"To Cape Cod."

"Why, Eleanor?"

"I ain't wanted," she said, her head low. "I made up my mind to go back to my own folks. I'm not going to be adopted any more."

David led her to the deep window-seat and made her sit facing him. He was too wise to attempt a caress with this issue between them.

"Do you think that's altogether fair to me?" he asked presently.

"I guess it won't make much difference to you. Something else will come along."

"Do you think it will be fair to your other aunts and uncles who have given so much care and thought to your welfare?"

"They'll get tired of their bargain."

"If they do get tired of their bargain it will be because they've turned out to be very poor sports. I've known every one of them a long time, and I've never known them to show any signs of poor sportsmanship yet. If you run away without giving them their chance to make good, it will be you who are the poor sport."

"She said you would marry and get tired of me, and I would have to go back to the country. If you marry and Uncle Jimmie marries—then Uncle Peter will marry, and—"

"You'd still have your Aunts Beulah and Margaret and Gertrude," David could not resist making the suggestion.

"They could do it, too. If one person broke up the vow, I guess they all would. Misfortunes never come singly."

"But even if we did, Eleanor, even if we all married, we'd still regard you as our own, our child, our charge."

"*She* said you wouldn't." The tears came now, and David gathered the little shaking figure to his breast. "I don't want to be the wife of the farmer for whom fate intended me," she sobbed. "I want to marry somebody refined with extravagant living and associations."

"That's one of the things we are bringing you up for, my dear." This aspect of the case occurred to David for the first time, but he realized its potency. "You mustn't take mother too seriously. Just jolly her along a little and you'll soon get to be famous friends. She's never had any little girls of her own, only my brother and me, and she doesn't know quite how to talk to them."

"The Hutchinsons had a hired butler and gold spoons, and they didn't think I was the dust beneath their feet. I don't know what to say to her. I said ain't, and I wasn't refined, and I'll only just be a disgrace to you. I'd rather go back to Cape Cod, and go out to work, and stand Albertina and everything."

"If you think it's the square thing to do," David said slowly, "you may go, Eleanor. I'll take you to New York to-morrow and get one of the girls to take you to Colhassett. Of course, if you do that it will put me in rather an awkward position. The others have all had you for two months and made good on the proposition. I shall have to admit that I couldn't even keep you with me twenty-four hours. Peter and Jimmie got along all right, but I couldn't handle you at all. As a cooperative parent, I'm such a failure that the whole experiment goes to pieces through me."

"Not you—her."

"Well, it's the same thing,—you couldn't stand the surroundings I brought you to. You couldn't even be polite to my mother for my sake."

"I—never thought of that, Uncle David."

"Think of it now for a few minutes, won't you, Eleanor?"

The rain was beginning to lash the windows, and to sweep the lawn in long slant strokes. The little girl held up her face as if it could beat through the panes on it.

"I thought," she said slowly, "that after Albertina I wouldn't *take* anything from anybody. Uncle Peter says that I'm just as good as anybody, even if I have been out to work. He said that all I had to do was just to stand up to people."

"There are a good many different ways of standing up to people, Eleanor. Be sure you've got the right way and then go ahead."

"I guess I ought to have been politer," Eleanor said slowly. "I ought to have thought that she was your own mother. You couldn't help the way she acted, o' course."

"The way you acted is the point, Eleanor."

Eleanor reflected.

"I'll act different if you want me to, Uncle David," she said, "and I won't go and leave you."

"That's my brave girl. I don't think that I altogether cover myself with glory in an interview with my mother," he added. "It isn't the thing that I'm best at, I admit."

"You did pretty good," Eleanor consoled him. "I guess she makes you kind of bashful the way she does me," from which David gathered with an odd sense of shock that Eleanor felt there was something to criticize in his conduct, if she had permitted herself to look for it.

"I know what I'll do," Eleanor decided dreamily with her nose against the pane. "I'll just pretend that she's Mrs. O'Farrel's aunt, and then whatever she does, I shan't care. I'll know that I'm the strongest and could hit her if I had a mind to, and then I shan't want to."

David contemplated her gravely for several seconds.

"By the time you grow up, Eleanor," he said finally, "you will have developed all your cooperative parents into fine strong characters. Your educational methods are wonderful."

"The dog got nearly drownded today in the founting," Eleanor wrote. "It is a very little dog about the size of Gwendolyn. It was out with Mademoiselle, and so was I, learning French on a garden seat. It teetered around on the edge of the big wash basin—the founting looks like a wash basin, and suddenly it fell in. I waded right in and got it, but it slipped around so I couldn't get it right away. It looked almost too dead to come to again, but I gave it first aid to the drownded the way Uncle Jimmie taught me to practicing on Gwendolyn. When I got it fixed I looked up and saw Uncle David's mother coming. I took the dog and gave it to her. I said, 'Madam, here's your dog.' Mademoiselle ran around ringing her hands and talking about it. Then I went up to Mrs. Bolling's room, and we talked. I told her how to make mustard pickles, and how my mother's grandpa's relation came over in the Mayflower, and about our single white lilac bush, and she's going to get one and make the pickles. Then I played double Canfield with her for a while. I'm glad I didn't go home before I knew her better. When she acts like Mrs. O'Farrel's aunt I pretend she is her, and we don't quarrel. She says does Uncle David go much to see Aunt Beulah, and I say, not so often as Uncle Jimmie does. Then she says does he go to see Aunt Margaret, and I say that he goes to see Uncle Peter the most. Well, if he doesn't he almost does. You can't tell Mrs. Madam Bolling that you won't tattle, because she would think the worst."

Eleanor grew to like Mademoiselle. She was the aging, rather wry faced Frenchwoman who had been David's young brother's governess and had made herself so useful to Mrs. Bolling that she was kept always on the place, half companion and half resident housekeeper. She was glad to have a child in charge again, and Eleanor soon found that her crooked features and severe high-shouldered back that had somewhat intimidated her at first, actually belonged to one of the kindest hearted creatures in the world.

Paris and Colhassett bore very little resemblance to each other, the two discovered. To be sure there were red geraniums every alternating year in the gardens of the Louvre, and every year in front of the Sunshine Library in Colhassett. The residents of both places did a great deal of driving in fine weather. In Colhassett they drove on the state highway, recently macadamized to the dismay of the taxpayers who did not own horses or automobiles. In Paris they drove out to the Bois by way of the Champs Elysees. In Colhassett they had only one ice-cream saloon, but in Paris they had a good many of them out-of-doors in the parks and even on the sidewalk, and there you could buy all kinds of sirups and 'what you call cordials' and *aperitifs*; but the two places on the whole were quite different. The people were different, too. The people of Colhassett were all religious and thought it was sinful to play cards on Sundays. Mademoiselle said she always felt wicked when she played them on a week day.

"I think of my mother," she said; "she would say 'Juliette, what will you say to the Lord when he knows that you have been playing cards on a working day. Playing cards is for Sunday.'"

"The Lord that they have in Colhassett is not like that," Eleanor stated without conscious irreverence.

"She is a vary fonny child, madam," Mademoiselle answered Mrs. Bolling's inquiry. "She has taste, but no—experience even of the most ordinary. She cooks, but she does no embroidery. She knits and knows no games to play. She has a good brain, but Mon Dieu, no one has taught her to ask questions with it."

"She has had lessons this year from some young Rogers graduates, very intelligent girls. I should think a year of that kind of training would have had its effect." Mrs. Bolling's finger went into every pie in her vicinity with unfailing direction.

"Lessons, yes, but no teaching. If she were not vary intelligent I think she would have suffered for it. The public schools they did somesing, but so little to elevate—to encourage."

Thus in a breath were Beulah's efforts as an educator disposed of.

"Would you like to undertake the teaching of that child for a year?" Mrs. Bolling asked thoughtfully.

"Oh! but yes, madam."

"I think I'll make the offer to David."

Mrs. Bolling was unsympathetic but she was thorough. She liked to see things properly done. Since David and his young friends had undertaken a venture so absurd, she decided to lend them a helping hand with it. Besides, now that she had no children of her own in the house, Mademoiselle was practically eating her head off. Also it had developed that David was fond of the child, so fond of her that to oppose that affection would have been bad policy, and Mrs. Bolling was politic when she chose to be. She chose to be politic now, for sometime during the season she was going to ask a very great favor of David, and she hoped, that by first being extraordinarily complaisant and kind and then by bringing considerable pressure to bear upon him, he would finally do what he was asked. The favor was to provide himself with a father-in-law, and that father-in-law the multi-millionaire parent of the raven-haired, crafty-eyed ingénue, who had begun angling for him that June night at the country club.

She made the suggestion to David on the eve of the arrival of all of Eleanor's guardians for the week-end. Mrs. Bolling had invited a house-party comprised of the associated parents as a part of her policy of kindness before the actual summoning of her forces for the campaign she was about to inaugurate.

David was really touched by his mother's generosity concerning Eleanor. He had been agreeably surprised at the development of the situation between the child and his mother. He had been obliged to go into town the day after Eleanor's first unfortunate encounter with her hostess, and had hurried home in fear and trembling to try to smooth out any tangles in the skein of their relationship that might have resulted from a day in each other's vicinity. After hurrying over the house and through the grounds in search of her he finally discovered the child companionably currying a damp and afflicted Pekinese in his mother's sitting-room, and engaged in a grave discussion of the relative merits of molasses and sugar as a sweetening for Boston baked beans.

It was while they were having their after-dinner coffee in the library, for which Eleanor had been allowed to come down, though nursery supper was the order of the day in the Bolling establishment, that David told his friends of his mother's offer.

"Of course, we decided to send her to school when she was twelve anyway," he said. "The idea was to keep her among ourselves for two years to establish the parental tie, or ties I should say. If she is quartered here with Mademoiselle we could still keep in touch with her and she would be having the advantage of a year's steady tuition under one person, and we'd be relieved—" a warning glance from Margaret, with an almost imperceptible inclination of her head in the direction of Beulah, caused him to modify the end of his sentence—"of the responsibility—for her physical welfare."

"Mentally and morally," Gertrude cut in, "the bunch would still supervise her entirely."

Jimmie, who was sitting beside her, ran his arm along the back of her chair affectionately, and then thought better of it and drew it away. He was, for some unaccountable reason, feeling awkward and not like himself. There was a girl in New York, with whom he was not in the least in love, who had recently taken it upon herself to demonstrate unmistakably that she was not in love with him. There was another girl who insisted on his writing her every day. Here was Gertrude, who never had any time for him any more, absolutely without enthusiasm at his proximity. He thought it would be a good idea to allow Eleanor to remain where she was and said so.

"Not that I won't miss the jolly times we had together, Babe," he said. "I was planning some real rackets this year,—to make up for what I put you through," he added in her ear, as she came and stood beside him for a minute.

Gertrude wanted to go abroad for a year, "and lick her wounds," as she told herself. She would have come back for her two months with Eleanor, but she was glad to be relieved of that necessity. Margaret had the secret feeling that the ordeal of the Hutchinsons was one that she would like to spare her foster child, and incidentally herself in relation to the adjustment of conditions necessary to Eleanor's visit. Peter wanted her with him, but he believed the new arrangement would be better for the child. Beulah alone held out for her rights and her parental privileges. The decision was finally left to Eleanor.

She stood in the center of the group a little forlornly while they awaited her word. A wave of her old shyness overtook her and she blushed hot and crimson.

"It's all in your own hands, dear," Beulah said briskly.

"Poor kiddie," Gertrude thought, "it's all wrong somehow."

"I don't know what you want me to say," Eleanor said piteously and sped to the haven of Peter's breast.

"We'll manage a month together anyway," Peter whispered.

"Then I guess I'll stay here," she whispered back, "because next I would have to go to Aunt Beulah's."

Peter, turning involuntarily in Beulah's direction, saw the look of chagrin and disappointment on her face, and realized how much she minded playing a losing part in the game and yet how well she was doing it. "She's only a straight-laced kid after all," he thought. "She's put her whole heart and soul into this thing. There's a look about the top part of her face when it's softened that's a little like Ellen's." Ellen was his dead fiancée—the girl in the photograph at home in his desk.

"I guess I'll stay here," Eleanor said aloud, "all in one place, and study with Mademoiselle."

It was a decision that, on the whole, she never regretted.

CHAPTER XIII

BROOK AND RIVER

"Standing with reluctant feet,
Where the brook and river meet."

"I think it's a good plan to put a quotation like Kipling at the top of the page whenever I write anything in this diary," Eleanor began in the smart leather bound book with her initials stamped in black on the red cover—the new private diary that had been Peter's gift to her on the occasion of her fifteenth birthday some months before. "I think it is a very expressive thing to do. The quotation above is one that expresses me, and I think it is beautiful too. Miss Hadley—that's my English teacher—the girls call her Haddock because she does look rather like a fish—says that it's undoubtedly one of the most poignant descriptions of adolescent womanhood ever made. I made a note to look up adolescent, but didn't. Bertha Stephens has my dictionary, and won't bring it back because the leaves are all stuck together with fudge, and she thinks she ought to buy me a new one. It is very honorable of her to feel that way, but she never will. Good old Stevie, she's a great borrower.

"'Neither a borrower nor a lender be,
For borrowing dulls the edge of husbandry.'

"Shakespeare.

"Well, I hardly know where to begin. I thought I would make a resumé of some of the events of the last year. I was only fourteen then, but still I did a great many things that might be of interest to me in my declining years when I look back into the annals of this book. To begin with I was only a freshie at Harmon. It is very different to be a sophomore. I can hardly believe that I was once a shivering looking little thing like all the freshmen that came in this year. I was very frightened, but did not think I showed it.

"'Oh! wad some power the giftie gie us,
To see ourselves as others see us.'

"Robert Burns had twins and a rather bad character, but after he met his bonnie Jean he wrote very beautiful poetry. A poet's life is usually sad anyhow—full of disappointment and pain—but I digress.

"I had two years with Mademoiselle at the Bollings' instead of one the way we planned. I haven't written in my Private Diary since the night of that momentous decision that I was to stay in one place instead of taking turns visiting my cooperative parents. I went to another school one year before I came to Harmon, and that brings me to the threshold of my fourteenth year. If I try to go back any farther, I'll never catch up. I spent that vacation with Aunt Margaret in a cottage on Long Island with her sister, and her sister's boy, who has grown up to be the silly kind that wants to kiss you and pull your hair, and those things. Aunt Margaret is so lovely I can't think of words to express it. 'Oh! rare pale Margaret,' as Tennyson says. She wears her hair in a coronet braid around the top of her head, and all her clothes are the color of violets or a soft dovey gray or white, though baby blue looks nice on her especially when she wears a fishyou.

"I went down to Cape Cod for a week before I came to Harmon, and while I was there my grandmother died. I can't write about that in this diary. I loved my grandmother and my grandmother loved me. Uncle Peter came, and took charge of everything. He has great strength that holds you up in trouble.

"The first day I came to Harmon I saw the girl I wanted for my best friend, and so we roomed together, and have done so ever since. Her name is Margaret Louise Hodges, but she is called Maggie Lou by every one. She has dark curly hair, and deep brown eyes, and a very silvery voice. I have found out that she lies some, but she says it is because she had such an unhappy childhood, and has promised to overcome it for my sake.

"That Christmas vacation the 'We Are Sevens' went up the Hudson to the Bollings' again, but that was the last time they ever went there. Uncle David and his mother had a terrible fight over them. I was sorry for Madam Bolling in a way. There was a girl she wanted Uncle David to marry, a rich girl who looked something like Cleopatra, very dark complexioned with burning eyes. She had a sweet little Pekinese something like Zaidee.

"Uncle David said that gold could never buy him, and to take her away, but Madam Bolling was very angry, of course. She accused him of wanting to marry Aunt Margaret, and called her a characterless, faded blonde. Then it was Uncle David's turn to get angry, and I have never seen any one get any angrier, and he told about the vow of celibacy, and how instead of having designs on him the whole crowd would back him up in his struggle to stay single. It was an awful row. I told Madam Bolling that I would help her to get Uncle David back, and I did, but she never forgave the other aunts and uncles. I suppose the feelings of a mother would prompt her to want Uncle David settled down with a rich and fashionable girl who would soon be the mother of a lot of lovely children. I can't imagine a Cleopatra looking baby, but she might have boys that looked like Uncle David.

"Vacations are really about all there is to school. Freshman year is mostly grinding and stuffing. Having six parents to send you boxes of 'grub' is better than having only two. Some of the girls are rather selfish about the eats, and come in and help themselves boldly when you are out of the room. Maggie Lou puts up signs over the candy box: 'Closed for Repairs,' or 'No Trespassing by Order of the Board of Health,' but they don't pay much attention. Well, last summer vacation I spent with Uncle Jimmie. I wouldn't tell this, but I reformed him. I made him sign the pledge. I don't know what pledge it was because I didn't read it, but he said he was addicted to something worse than anything I could think of, and if somebody didn't pull him up, he wouldn't answer for the consequences. I asked him why he didn't choose Aunt Gertrude to do it, and he groaned only. So I said to write out a pledge, and sign it and I would be the witness. We were at a hotel with his brother's family. It isn't proper any more for me to go around with my uncles unless I have a chaperon. Mademoiselle says that I oughtn't even to go downtown alone with them but, of course, that is French etiquette, and not American. Well, there were lots of pretty girls at this hotel, all wearing white and pink dresses, and carrying big bell shaped parasols of bright colors. They looked sweet, like so many flowers, but Uncle Jimmie just about hated the sight of them. He said they were not girls at all, but just pink and white devices of the devil. On the whole he didn't act much like my merry uncle, but we had good times together playing tennis and golf, and going on parties with his brother's family, all mere children but the mother and father. Uncle Jimmie was afraid to go and get his mail all summer, although he had a great many letters on blue and lavender note paper scented with Roger et Gallet's violet, and Hudnut's carnation. We used to go down to the beach and make bonfires and burn them unread, and then toast marshmallows in their ashes. He said that they were communications from the spirits of the dead. I should have thought that they were from different girls, but he seemed to hate the sight of girls so much. Once I asked him if he had ever had an unhappy love-affair, just to see what he would say, but he replied 'no, they had all been happy ones,' and groaned and groaned.

"Aunt Beulah has changed too. She has become a suffragette and thinks only of getting women their rights and their privileges.

"Maggie Lou is an anti, and we have long arguments about the cause. She says that woman's place is in the home, but I say look at me, who have no home, how can I wash and bake and brew like the women of my grandfather's day, visiting around the way I do? And she says that it is the principle of the thing that is involved, and I ought to take a stand for or against. Everybody has so many different arguments that I don't know what I think yet, but some day I shall make up my mind for good.

"Well, that about brings me up to the present. I meant to describe a few things in detail, but I guess I will not begin on the past in that way. I don't get so awfully much time to write in this diary because of the many interruptions of school life, and the way the monitors snoop in study hours.

I don't know who I am going to spend my Christmas holidays with. I sent Uncle Peter a poem three days ago, but he has not answered it yet. I'm afraid he thought it was very silly. I don't hardly know what it means myself. It goes as follows:

"A Song

"The moon is very pale to-night,
The summer wind swings high,
I seek the temple of delight,
And feel my love draw nigh.

"I seem to feel his fragrant breath
Upon my glowing cheek.
Between us blows the wind of death,—
I shall not hear him speak.

"I don't know why I like to write love poems, but most of the women poets did. This one made me cry."

CHAPTER XIV

Margaret in mauve velvet and violets, and Gertrude in a frock of smart black and white were in the act of meeting by appointment at Sherry's one December afternoon, with a comfortable cup of tea in mind. Gertrude emerged from the recess of the revolving door and Margaret, sitting eagerly by the entrance, almost upset the attendant in her rush to her friend's side.

"Oh! Gertrude," she cried, "I'm so glad to see you. My family is trying to cut me up in neat little quarters and send me north, south, east and west, for the Christmas holidays, and I want to stay home and have Eleanor. How did I ever come to be born into a family of giants, tell me that, Gertrude?"

"The choice of parents is thrust upon us at an unfortunately immature period, I'll admit," Gertrude laughed. "My parents are dears, but they've never forgiven me for being an artist instead of a dubby bud. Shall we have tea right away or shall we sit down and discuss life?"

"Both," Margaret said. "I don't know which is the hungrier—flesh or spirit."

But as they turned toward the dining-room a familiar figure blocked their progress.

"I thought that was Gertrude's insatiable hat," David exclaimed delightedly. "I've phoned for you both until your families have given instructions that I'm not to be indulged any more. I've got a surprise for you.—Taxi," he said to the man at the door.

"Not till we've had our tea," Margaret wailed. "You couldn't be so cruel, David."

"You shall have your tea, my dear, and one of the happiest surprises of your life into the bargain," David assured her as he led the way to the waiting cab.

"I wouldn't leave this place unfed for anybody but you, David, not if it were ever so, and then some, as Jimmie says."

"What's the matter with Jimmie, anyhow?" David inquired as the taxi turned down the Avenue and immediately entangled itself in a hopeless mesh of traffic.

"I don't know; why?" Gertrude answered, though she had not been the one addressed at the moment. "What's the matter with this hat?" she rattled on without waiting for an answer. "I thought it was good-looking myself, and Madam Paran robbed me for it."

"It is good-looking," David allowed. "It seems to be a kind of retrieving hat, that's all. Keeps you in a rather constant state of looking after the game."

"What about my hat, David?" Margaret inquired anxiously. "Do you like that?"

"I do," David admitted. "I'm crazy about it. It's a lovely cross between the style affected by the late Emperor Napoleon and my august grandmother, with some frills added."

The chauffeur turned into a cross street and stopped abruptly before an imposing but apparently unguarded entrance.

"Why, I thought this was a studio building," Gertrude said. "David, if you're springing a tea party on us, and we in the wild ungovernable state we are at present, I'll shoot the way my hat is pointing."

"Straight through my left eye-glass," David finished. "You wait till you see the injustice you have done me."

But Margaret, who often understood what was happening a few moments before the revelation of it, clutched at his elbow.

"Oh! David, David," she whispered, "how wonderful!"

"Wait till you see," David said, and herded them into the elevator.

Their destination was the top floor but one. David hurried them around the bend in the sleekly carpeted corridor and touched the bell on the right of the first door they came to. It opened almost instantly and David's man, who was French, stood bowing and smiling on the threshold.

"Mr. Styvvisont has arrive'," he said; "he waits you."

"Welcome to our city," Peter cried, appearing in the doorway of the room Alphonse was indicating with that high gesture of delight with which only a Frenchman can lead the way. "Jimmie's coming up from the office and Beulah's due any minute. What do you think of the place, girls?"

"Is it really yours, David?"

"Surest thing you know." He grinned like a schoolboy. "It's really ours, that's what it is. I've broken away from the mater at last," he added a little sheepishly. "I'm going to work seriously. I've got an all-day desk job in my uncle's office and I'm going to dig in and see what I can make of myself. Also, this is going to be our headquarters, and Eleanor's permanent home if we're all agreed upon it,—but look around, ladies. Don't spare my blushes. If you think I can interior decorate, just tell me so frankly. This is the living-room."

"It's like that old conundrum—black and white and red all over," Gertrude said. "I never saw anything so stunning in all my life."

"Gosh! I admire your nerve," Peter cried, "papering this place in white, and then getting in all this heavy carved black stuff, and the red in the tapestries and screens and pillows."

"I wanted it to look studioish a little," David explained, "I wanted to get away from Louis Quartorze."

"And drawing-rooms like mother used to make," Gertrude suggested. "I like your Oriental touches. Do you see, Margaret, everything is Indian or Chinese? The ubiquitous Japanese print is conspicuous by its absence."

"I've got two portfolios full of 'em," David said, "and I always have one or two up in the bedrooms. I change 'em around, you know, the way the Japs do themselves, a different scene every few days and the rest decently out of sight till you're ready for 'em."

"It's like a fairy story," Margaret said.

"I thought you'd appreciate what little Arabian Nights I was able to introduce. I bought that screen," he indicated a sweep of Chinese line and color, "with my eye on you, and that Aladdin's lamp is yours, of course. You're to come in here and rub it whenever you like, and your heart's desire will instantly be vouchsafed to you."

"What will Eleanor say?" Peter suggested, as David led the way through the corridor and up the tiny stairs which led to the more intricate part of the establishment. "This is her room, didn't you say, David?" He paused on the threshold of a bedroom done in ivory white and yellow, with all its hangings of a soft golden silk.

"She once said that she wanted a yellow room," David said, "a daffy-down-dilly room, and I've tried to get her one. I know last year that Maggie Lou child refused to have yellow curtains in that flatiron shaped sitting-room of theirs, and Eleanor refused to be comforted."

A wild whoop in the below stairs announced Jimmie; and Beulah arrived simultaneously with the tea tray. Jimmie was ecstatic when the actual function of the place was explained to him.

"Headquarters is the one thing we've lacked," he said; "a place of our own, hully gee! It makes me feel almost human again."

"You haven't been feeling altogether human lately, have you, Jimmie?" Margaret asked over her tea cup.

"No, dear, I haven't." Jimmie flashed her a grateful smile. "I'm a bad egg," he explained to her darkly, "and the only thing you can do with me is to scramble me."

"Scrambled is just about the way I should have described your behavior of late,—but that's Gertrude's line," David said. "Only she doesn't seem to be taking an active part in the conversation. Aren't you Jimmie's keeper any more, Gertrude?"

"Not since she's come back from abroad," Jimmie muttered without looking at her.

"Eleanor's taken the job over now," Peter said. "She's made him swear off red ink and red neckties."

"Any color so long's it's red is the color that suits me best," Jimmie quoted. "Lord, isn't this room a pippin?" He swam in among the bright pillows of the divan and so hid his face for a moment. It had been a good many weeks since he had seen Gertrude.

"I want to give a suffrage tea here," Beulah broke in suddenly. "It's so central, but I don't suppose David would hear of it."

"Angels and Ministers of Grace defend us—" Peter began.

"My *mother* would hear of it," David said, "and then there wouldn't be any little studio any more. She doesn't believe in votes for women."

"How any woman in this day and age—" Beulah began, and thought better of it, since she was discussing Mrs. Bolling.

"Makes your blood boil, doesn't it—Beulahland?" Gertrude suggested helpfully, reaching for the tea cakes. "Never mind, I'll vote for women. I'll march in your old peerade."

"The Lord helps those that help themselves," Peter said, "that's why Gertrude is a suffragist. She believes in helping herself, in every sense, don't you, 'Trude?"

"Not quite in every sense," Gertrude said gravely. "Sometimes I feel like that girl that Margaret describes as caught in a horrid way between two generations. I'm neither old-fashioned nor modern."

"I'd rather be that way than early Victorian," Margaret sighed.

"Speaking of the latest generation, has anybody any objection to having our child here for the holidays?" David asked. "My idea is to have one grand Christmas dinner. I suppose we'll all have to eat one meal with our respective families, but can't we manage to get together here for dinner at night? Don't you think that we could?"

"We can't, but we will," Margaret murmured. "Of course, have Eleanor here. I wanted her with me but the family thought otherwise. They've been trying to send me away for my health, David."

"Well, they shan't. You'll stay in New York for your health and come to my party."

"Margaret's health is merely a matter of Margaret's happiness anyhow. Her soul and her body are all one," Gertrude said.

"Then cursed be he who brings anything but happiness to Margaret," Peter said, to which sentiment David added a solemn "Amen."

"I wish you wouldn't," Margaret said, shivering a little, "I feel as if some one were—were—"

"Trampling the violets on your grave," Gertrude finished for her.

Christmas that year fell on a Monday, and Eleanor did not leave school till the Friday before the great day. Owing to the exigencies of the holiday season none of her guardians came to see her before the dinner party itself. Even David was busy with his mother—installed now for a few weeks in the hotel suite that would be her home until the opening of the season at Palm Beach—and had only a few hurried words with her. Mademoiselle, whom he had imported for the occasion, met her at the station and helped her to do her modest shopping which consisted chiefly of gifts for her beloved aunts and uncles. She had arranged these things lovingly at their plates, and fled to dress when they began to assemble for the celebration. The girls were the first arrivals. Then Peter.

"How's our child, David?" Gertrude asked. "I had a few minutes' talk with her over the telephone and she seemed to be flourishing."

"She is," David answered. "She's grown several feet since we last saw her. They've been giving scenes from Shakespeare at school and she's been playing Juliet, it appears. She has had a fight with another girl about suffrage—I don't know which side she was on, Beulah, I am merely giving you the facts as they came to me—and the other girl was so unpleasant about it that she has been visited by just retribution in the form of the mumps, and had to be sent home and quarantined."

"Sounds a bit priggish," Peter suggested.

"Not really," David said, "she's as sound as a nut. She's only going through the different stages."

"To pass deliberately through one's ages," Beulah quoted, "is to get the heart out of a liberal education."

"Bravo, Beulah," Gertrude cried, "you're quite in your old form to-night."

"Is she just the same little girl, David?" Margaret asked.

"Just the same. She really seems younger than ever. I don't know why she doesn't come down. There she is, I guess. No, it's only Alphonse letting in Jimmie."

Jimmie, whose spirits seemed to have revived under the holiday influence, was staggering under the weight of his parcels. The Christmas presents had already accumulated to a considerable mound on the couch. Margaret was brooding over them and trying not to look greedy. She was still very much of a child herself in relation to Santa Claus.

"Merry Christmas!" Jimmie cried. "Where's my child?"

"Coming," David said.

"Look at the candy kids. My eyes—but you're a slick trio, girls. Pale lavender, pale blue, and pale pink, and all quite sophisticatedly décolleté. You go with the decorations, too. I don't know quite why you do, but you do."

"Give honor where honor is due, dearie. That's owing to the cleverness of the decorator," David said.

"No man calls me dearie and lives to tell the tale," Jimmie remarked almost dreamily as he squared off. "How'll you have it, Dave?"

But at that instant there was an unexpected interruption. Alphonse threw open the big entrance door at the farther end of the long room with a flourish.

"Mademoiselle Juliet Capulet," he proclaimed with the grand air, and then retired behind his hand, smiling broadly.

Framed in the high doorway, complete, cap and curls, softly rounding bodice, and the long, straight lines of the Renaissance, stood Juliet—Juliet, immemorial, immortal, young—austerely innocent and delicately shy, already beautiful, and yet potential of all the beauty and the wisdom of the world.

"I've never worn these clothes before anybody but the girls before," Eleanor said, "but I thought"—she looked about her appealingly—"you might like it—for a surprise."

"Great jumping Jehoshaphat," Jimmie exclaimed, "I thought you said she was the same little girl, David."

"She was half an hour ago," David answered, "I never saw such a metamorphosis. In fact, I don't think I ever saw Juliet before."

"She is the thing itself," Gertrude answered, the artist in her sobered by the vision.

But Peter passed a dazed hand over his eyes and stared at the delicate figure advancing to him.

"My God! she's a woman," he said, and drew the hard breath of a man just awakened from sleep.

"I thought"—she looked about her appealingly—"you might like it—for a surprise"

CHAPTER XV

"Dear Uncle Jimmie:

"It was a pleasant surprise to get letters from every one of my uncles the first week I got back to school. It was unprecedented. You wrote me two letters last year, Uncle David six, and Uncle Peter sixteen. He is the best correspondent, but perhaps that is because I ask him the most advice. The Christmas party was lovely. I shall never forget the expressions on all the different faces when I came down in my Juliet suit. I thought at first that no one liked me in it, but I guess they did.

"You know how well I liked my presents because you heard my wild exclamations of delight. I never had such a nice Christmas. It was sweet of the We Are Sevens to get me that ivory set, and to know that every different piece was the loving thought of a different aunt or uncle. I love the yellow monogram. It looks entirely unique, and I like to have things that are not like anybody else's in the world, don't you, Uncle Jimmie? I am glad you liked your cuff links. They are 'neat,' but not 'gaudy.' You play golf so well I thought a golf stick was a nice emblem for you, and would remind you of me and last summer.

"I am glad you think it is easier to keep your pledge now. I made a New Year's resolution to go without chocolates, and give the money they would cost to some good cause, but it's hard to pick out a cause, or to decide exactly how much money you are saving. I can eat the chocolates that are sent to me, however!!!!

"Uncle David said that he thought you were not like yourself lately, but you seemed just the same to me Christmas, only more affectionate. I love you very much. I was really only joking about the chocolates. Eleanor."

"Dear Uncle David:

"I was glad to get your nice letter. You did not have to write in response to my bread and butter letter, but I am glad you did. When I am at school, and getting letters all the time I feel as if I were living two beautiful lives all at once, the life of a 'cooperative child' and the life of Eleanor Hamlin, schoolgirl, both together. Letters make the people you love seem very near to you, don't you think they do? I sleep with all my letters under my pillow whenever I feel the least little bit homesick, and they almost seem to breathe sometimes.

"School is the same old school. Maggie Lou had a wrist watch, too, for Christmas, but not so pretty as the one you gave me. Miss Hadley says I do remarkable work in English whenever I feel like it. I don't know whether that's a compliment or not. I took Kris Kringle for the subject of a theme the other day, and represented him as caught in an iceberg in the grim north, and not being able to reach all the poor little children in the tenements and hovels. The Haddock said it showed imagination.

"There was a lecture at school on Emerson the other day. The speaker was a noted literary lecturer from New York. He had wonderful waving hair, more like Pader—I can't spell him, but you know who I mean—than Uncle Jimmie's, but a little like both. He introduced some very noble thoughts in his discourse, putting perfectly old ideas in a new way that made you think a lot more of them. I think a tall man like that with waving hair can do a great deal of good as a lecturer, because you listen a good deal more respectfully than if they were plain looking. His voice sounded a good deal like what I imagine Romeo's voice did. I had a nice letter from Madam Bolling. I love you, and I have come to the bottom of the sheet. Eleanor."

"Dear Uncle Peter:

"I have just written to my other uncles, so I won't write you a long letter this time. They deserve letters because of being so unusually prompt after the holidays. You always deserve letters, but not specially now, any more than any other time.

"Uncle Peter, I wrote to my grandfather. It seems funny to think of Albertina's aunt taking care of him now that Grandma is gone. I suppose Albertina is there a lot. She sent me a post card for Christmas. I didn't send her any.

"Uncle Peter, I miss my grandmother out of the world. I remember how I used to take care of her, and put a soapstone in the small of her back when she was cold. I wish sometimes that I could hold your hand, Uncle Peter, when I get thinking about it.

"Well, school is the same old school. Bertha Stephens has a felon on her finger, and that lets her out of hard work for a while. I will enclose a poem suggested by a lecture I heard recently on Emerson. It isn't very good, but it will help to fill up the envelope. I love you, and love you. Eleanor.

"Life

"Life is a great, a noble task,

When we fulfill our duty.
To work, that should be all we ask,
And seek the living beauty.
We know not whence we come, or where
Our dim pathway is leading,
Whether we tread on lilies fair,
Or trample love-lies-bleeding.
But we must onward go and up,
Nor stop to question whither.
E'en if we drink the bitter cup,
And fall at last, to wither.

"P. S. I haven't got the last verse very good yet, but I think the second one is pretty. You know 'love-lies-bleeding' is a flower, but it sounds allegorical the way I have put it in. Don't you think so? You know what all the crosses stand for."

Eleanor's fifteenth year was on the whole the least eventful year of her life, though not by any means the least happy. She throve exceedingly, and gained the freedom and poise of movement and spontaneity that result from properly balanced periods of work and play and healthful exercise. From being rather small of her age she developed into a tall slender creature, inherently graceful and erect, with a small, delicate head set flower-wise on a slim white neck. Gertrude never tired of modeling that lovely contour, but Eleanor herself was quite unconscious of her natural advantages. She preferred the snappy-eyed, stocky, ringleted type of beauty, and spent many unhappy quarters of an hour wishing she were pretty according to the inexorable ideals of Harmon.

She spent her vacation at David's apartment in charge of Mademoiselle, though the latter part of the summer she went to Colhassett, quite by herself according to her own desire, and spent a month with her grandfather, now in charge of Albertina's aunt. She found Albertina grown into a huge girl, sunk in depths of sloth and snobbishness, who plied her with endless questions concerning life in the gilded circles of New York society. Eleanor found her disgusting and yet possessed of that vague fascination that the assumption of prerogative often carries with it.

She found her grandfather very old and shrunken, yet perfectly taken care of and with every material want supplied. She realized as she had never done before how the faithful six had assumed the responsibility of this household from the beginning, and how the old people had been warmed and comforted by their bounty. She laughed to remember her simplicity in believing that an actual salary was a perquisite of her adoption, and understood for the first time how small a part of the expense of their living this faithful stipend had defrayed. She looked back incredulously on that period when she had lived with them in a state of semi-starvation on the corn meal and cereals and very little else that her dollar and a half a week had purchased, and the "garden sass," that her grandfather had faithfully hoed and tended in the straggling patch of plowed field that he would hoe and tend no more. She spent a month practically at his feet, listening to his stories, helping him to find his pipe and tobacco and glasses, and reading the newspaper to him, and felt amply rewarded by his final acknowledgment that she was a good girl and he would as soon have her come again whenever she felt like it.

On her way back to school she spent a week with her friend, Margaret Louise, in the Connecticut town where she lived with her comfortable, commonplace family. It was while she was on this visit that the most significant event of the entire year took place, though it was a happening that she put out of her mind as soon as possible and never thought of it again when she could possibly avoid it.

Maggie Lou had a brother of seventeen, and one night in the corner of a moonlit porch, when they happened to be alone for a half hour, he had asked Eleanor to kiss him.

"I don't want to kiss you," Eleanor said. Then, not wishing to convey a sense of any personal dislike to the brother of a friend to whom she was so sincerely devoted, she added, "I don't know you well enough."

He was a big boy, with mocking blue eyes and rough tweed clothes that hung on him loosely.

"When you know me better, will you let me kiss you?" he demanded.

"I don't know," Eleanor said, still endeavoring to preserve the amenities.

He took her hand and played with it softly.

"You're an awful sweet little girl," he said.

"I guess I'll go in now."

"Sit still. Sister'll be back in a minute." He pulled her back to the chair from which she had half arisen. "Don't you believe in kissing?"

"I don't believe in kissing *you*," she tried to say, but the words would not come. She could only pray for deliverance through the arrival of some member of the family. The boy's face was close to hers. It looked sweet in the moonlight she thought. She wished he would talk of something else besides kissing.

"Don't you like me?" he persisted.

"Yes, I do." She was very uncomfortable.

"Well, then, there's no more to be said." His lips sought hers and pressed them. His breath came heavily, with little irregular catches in it.

She pushed him away and turned into the house.

"Don't be angry, Eleanor," he pleaded, trying to snatch at her hand.

"I'm not angry," she said, her voice breaking, "I just wish you hadn't, that's all."

There was no reference to this incident in the private diary, but, with an instinct which would have formed an indissoluble bond between herself and her Uncle Jimmie, she avoided dimly lit porches and boys with mischievous eyes and broad tweed covered shoulders.

For her guardians too, this year was comparatively smooth running and colorless. Beulah's militant spirit sought the assuagement of a fierce expenditure of energy on the work that came to her hand through her new interest in suffrage. Gertrude flung herself into her sculpturing. She had been hurt as only the young can be hurt when their first delicate desires come to naught. She was very warm-blooded and eager under her cool veneer, and she had spent four years of hard work and hungry yearning for the fulness of a life she was too constrained to get any emotional hold on. Her fancy for Jimmie she believed was quite over and done with.

Margaret, warmed by secret fires and nourished by the stuff that dreams are made of, flourished strangely in her attic chamber, and learned the wisdom of life by some curious method of her own of apprehending its dangers and delights. The only experiences she had that year were two proposals of marriage, one from a timid professor of the romance languages and the other from a young society man, already losing his waist line, whose sensuous spirit had been stirred by the ethereal grace of hers; but these things interested her very little. She was the princess, spinning fine dreams and waiting for the dawning of the golden day when the prince should come for her. Neither she nor Gertrude ever gave a serious thought to the five-year-old vow of celibacy, which was to Beulah as real and as binding as it had seemed on the first day she took it.

Peter and David and Jimmie went their own way after the fashion of men, all of them identified with the quickening romance of New York business life. David in Wall Street was proving to be something of a financier to his mother's surprise and amazement; and the pressure relaxed, he showed some slight initiative in social matters. In fact, two mothers, who were on Mrs. Bolling's list as suitable parents-in-law, took heart of grace and began angling for him adroitly, while their daughters served him tea and made unabashed, modern-débutante eyes at him.

Jimmie, successfully working his way up to the top of his firm, suffered intermittently from his enthusiastic abuse of the privileges of liberty and the pursuit of happiness. His mind and soul were in reality hot on the trail of a wife, and there was no woman among those with whom he habitually foregathered whom his spirit recognized as his own woman. He was further rendered helpless and miserable by the fact that he had not the slightest idea of his trouble. He regarded himself as a congenital Don Juan, from whom his better self shrank at times with a revulsion of loathing.

Peter felt that he had his feet very firmly on a rather uninspired earth. He was getting on in the woolen business, which happened to be the vocation his father had handed down to him. He belonged to an amusing club, and he still felt himself irrevocably widowed by the early death of the girl in the photograph he so faithfully cherished. Eleanor was a very vital interest in his life. It had seemed to him for a few minutes at the Christmas party that she was no longer the little girl he had known, that a lovelier, more illusive creature—a woman—had come to displace her, but when she had flung her arms around him he had realized that it was still the heart of a child beating so fondly against his own.

The real trouble with arrogating to ourselves the privileges of parenthood is that our native instincts are likely to become deflected by the substitution of the artificial for the natural responsibility. Both Peter and David had the unconscious feeling that their obligation to their race was met by their communal interest in Eleanor. Beulah, of course, sincerely believed that the filling in of an intellectual concept of life was all that was required of her. Only Jimmie groped blindly and bewilderedly for his own. Gertrude and Margaret both understood that they were unnaturally alone in a world where lovers met and mated, but they, too, hugged to their souls the flattering unction that they were parents of a sort.

Thus three sets of perfectly suitable and devoted young men and women, of marriageable age, with dozens of interests and sympathies in common, and one extraordinarily vital bond, continued to walk side by side in a state of inhuman preoccupation, their gaze fixed inward instead of upon one another; and no Divine Power, happening upon the curious circumstance, believed the matter one for His intervention nor stooped to take the respective puppets by the back of their unconscious necks, and so knock their sluggish heads together.

CHAPTER XVI

"I am sixteen years and eight months old to-day," Eleanor wrote, "and I have had the kind of experience that makes me feel as if I never wanted to be any older. I know life is full of disillusionment and pain, but I did not know that any one with whom you have broken bread, and slept in the same room with, and told everything to for four long years, could turn out to be an absolute traitor and villainess. Let me begin at the beginning. For nearly a year now I have noticed that Bertha Stephens avoided me, and presented the appearance of disliking me. I don't like to have any one dislike me, and I have tried to do little things for her that would win back her affection, but with no success. As I was editing the Lantern I could print her essayettes (as she called them) and do her lots of little favors in a literary way, which she seemed to appreciate, but personally she avoided me like the plague.

"Of course Stevie has lots of faults, and since Margaret Louise and I always talked everything over we used to talk about Stevie in the same way. I remember that she used to try to draw me out about Stevie's character. I've always thought Stevie was a kind of piker, that is that she would say she was going to do a thing, and then from sheer laziness not do it. My dictionary was a case in point. She gummed it all up with her nasty fudge and then wouldn't give it back to me or get me another, but the reason she wouldn't give it back to me was because her feelings were too fine to return a damaged article, and not fine enough to make her hump herself and get me another. That's only one kind of a piker and not the worst kind, but it was *pikerish*.

"All this I told quite frankly to Maggie—I mean Margaret Louise, because I had no secrets from her and never thought there was any reason why I shouldn't. Stevie has a horrid brother, also, who has been up here to dances. All the girls hate him because he is so spoony. He isn't as spoony as Margaret Louise's brother, but he's quite a sloppy little spooner at that. Well, I told Margaret Louise that I didn't like Stevie's brother, and then I made the damaging remark that one reason I didn't like him was because he looked so much like Stevie. I didn't bother to explain to Maggie—I will not call her Maggie Lou any more, because that is a dear little name and sounds so affectionate,—Margaret Louise—what I meant by this, because I thought it was perfectly evident. Stevie is a peachy looking girl, a snow white blonde with pinky cheeks and dimples. Well, her brother is a snow white blond too, and he has pinky cheeks and dimples and his name is Carlo! We, of course, at once named him Curlo. It is not a good idea for a man to look too much like his sister, or to have too many dimples in his chin and cheeks. I had only to think of him in the same room with my three uncles to get his number exactly. I don't mean to use slang in my diary, but I can't seem to help it. Professor Mathews says that slang has a distinct function in the language— in replenishing it, but Uncle Peter says about slang words, that 'many are called, and few are chosen,' and there is no need to try to accommodate them all in one's vocabulary.

"Well, I told Margaret Louise all these things about Curlo, and how he tried to hold my hand coming from the station one day, when the girls all went up to meet the boys that came up for the dance,—and I told her everything else in the world that happened to come into my head.

"Then one day I got thinking about leaving Harmon—this is our senior year, of course—and I thought that I should leave all the girls with things just about right between us, excepting good old Stevie, who had this queer sort of grouch against me. So I decided that I'd just go around and have it out with her, and I did. I went into her room one day when her roommate was out, and demanded a show down. Well, I found out that Maggie—Margaret Louise had just repeated to Stevie every living thing that I ever said about her, just as I said it, only without the explanations and foot-notes that make any kind of conversation more understandable.

"Stevie told me all these things one after another, without stopping, and when she was through I wished that the floor would open and swallow me up, but nothing so comfortable happened. I was obliged to gaze into Stevie's overflowing eyes and own up to the truth as well as I could, and explain it. It was the most humiliating hour that I ever spent, but I told Stevie exactly what I felt about her 'nothing extenuate, and naught set down in malice,' and what I had said about her to our mutual friend, who by the way, is not the mutual friend of either of us any longer. We were both crying by the time I had finished, but we understood each other. There were one or two things that she said she didn't think she would ever forget that I had said about her, but even those she could forgive. She said that my dislike of her had rankled in her heart so long that it took away all the bitterness to know that I wasn't really her enemy. She said that my coming to her that way, and not lying had showed that I had lots of character, and she thought in time that we could be quite intimate friends if I wanted to as much as she did.

"After my talk with Stevie I still hoped against hope that Margaret Louise would turn out to have some reason or excuse for what she had done. I knew she had done it, but when a thing like that happens that upsets your whole trust in a person you simply can not believe the evidence of your own senses. When you read of a situation like that in a book you are all prepared for it by the author, who has taken the trouble to explain the moral weakness or unpleasantness of the character, and given you to understand that you are to expect a betrayal from him or her; but when it happens in real life out of a clear sky you have nothing to go upon that makes you even *believe* what you know.

"I won't even try to describe the scene that occurred between Margaret Louise and me. She cried and she lied, and she accused me of trying to curry favor with Stevie, and Stevie of being a backbiter, and she argued and argued about all kinds of things but the truth, and when I tried to pin her down to it, she ducked and crawled and sidestepped in a way that was dreadful. I've seen her do something like it before about different things, and I ought to have known then what she was like inside of her soul, but I guess you have to be the object of such a scene before you realize the full force of it.

"All I said was, 'Margaret Louise, if that's all you've got to say about the injury you have done me, then everything is over between us from this minute;' and it was, too.

"I feel as if I had been writing a beautiful story or poem on what I thought was an enduring tablet of marble, and some one had come and wiped it all off as if it were mere scribblings on a slate. I don't know whether it would seem like telling tales to tell Uncle Peter or not; I don't quite know whether I want to tell him. Sometimes I wish I had a mother to tell such things to. It seems to me that a real mother would know what to say that would help you. Disillusion is a very strange thing—like death, only having people die seems more natural somehow. When they die you can remember the happy hours that you spent with them, but when disillusionment comes then you have lost even your beautiful memories.

"We had for the subject of our theme this week, 'What Life Means to Me,' which of course was the object of many facetious remarks from the girls, but I've been thinking that if I sat down seriously to state in just so many words what life means to *me*, I hardly know what I would transcribe. It means disillusionment and death for one thing. Since my grandfather died last year I have had nobody left of my own in the world,—no real blood relation. Of course, I am a good deal fonder of my aunts and uncles than most people are of their own flesh and blood, but own flesh and blood is a thing that it makes you feel shivery to be without. If I had been Margaret Louise's own flesh and blood, she would never have acted like that to me. Stevie stuck up for Carlo as if he was really something to be proud of. Perhaps my uncles and aunts feel that way about me, I don't know. I don't even know if I feel that way about them. I certainly criticize them in my soul at times, and feel tired of being dragged around from pillar to post. I don't feel that way about Uncle Peter, but there is nobody else that I am certain, positive sure that I love better than life itself. If there is only one in the world that you feel that way about, I might not be Uncle Peter's one.

"Oh! I wish Margaret Louise had not sold her birthright for a mess of pottage. I wish I had a home that I had a perfect right to go and live in forevermore. I wish my mother was here to comfort me to-night."

CHAPTER XVII

A Real Kiss

At seventeen, Eleanor was through at Harmon. She was to have one year of preparatory school and then it was the desire of Beulah's heart that she should go to Rogers. The others contended that the higher education should be optional and not obligatory. The decision was finally to be left to Eleanor herself, after she had considered it in all its bearings.

"If she doesn't decide in favor of college," David said, "and she makes her home with me here, as I hope she will do, of course, I don't see what society we are going to be able to give her. Unfortunately none of our contemporaries have growing daughters. She ought to meet eligible young men and that sort of thing."

"Not yet," Margaret cried. The two were having a cozy cup of tea at his apartment. "You're so terribly worldly, David, that you frighten me sometimes."

"You don't know where I will end, is that the idea?"

"I don't know where Eleanor will end, if you're already thinking of eligible young men for her."

"Those things have got to be thought of," David answered gravely.

"I suppose they have," Margaret sighed. "I don't want her to be married. I want to take her off by myself and growl over her all alone for a while. Then I want Prince Charming to come along and snatch her up quickly, and set her behind his milk white charger and ride away with her. If we've all got to get together and connive at marrying her off there won't be any comfort in having her."

"I don't know," David said thoughtfully; "I think that might be fun, too. A vicarious love-affair that you can manipulate is one of the most interesting games in the world."

"That's not my idea of an interesting game," Margaret said. "I like things very personal, David,—you ought to know that by this time."

"I do know that," David said, "but it sometimes occurs to me that except for a few obvious facts of that nature I really know very little about you, Margaret."

"There isn't much to know—except that I'm a woman."

"That's a good deal," David answered slowly; "to a mere man that seems to be considerable of an adventure."

"It is about as much of an adventure sometimes as it would be to be a field of clover in an insectless world.—This is wonderful tea, David, but your cream is like butter and floats around in it in wudges. No, don't get any more, I've got to go home. Grandmother still thinks it's very improper for me to call upon you, in spite of Mademoiselle and your ancient and honorable housekeeper."

"Don't go," David said; "I apologize on my knees for the cream. I'll send out and have it wet down, or whatever you do to cream in that state. I want to talk to you. What did you mean by your last remark?"

"About the cream, or the proprieties?"

"About women."

"Everything and nothing, David dear. I'm a little bit tired of being one, that's all, and I want to go home."

"She wants to go home when she's being so truly delightful and cryptic," David said. "Have you been seeing visions, Margaret, in my hearth fire? Your eyes look as if you had."

"I thought I did for a minute." She rose and stood absently fitting her gloves to her fingers. "I don't know exactly what it was I saw, but it was something that made me uncomfortable. It gives me the creeps to talk about being a woman. David, do you know sometimes I have a kind of queer hunch about Eleanor? I love her, you know, dearly, dearly. I think that she is a very successful kind of Frankenstein; but there are moments when I have the feeling that she's going to be a storm center and bring some queer trouble upon us. I wouldn't say this to anybody but you, David."

As David tucked her in the car—he had arrived at the dignity of owning one now—and watched her sweet silhouette disappear, he, too, had his moment of clairvoyance. He felt that he was letting something very precious slip out of sight, as if some radiant and delicate gift had been laid lightly within his grasp and as lightly withdrawn again. As if when the door closed on his friend Margaret some stranger, more silent creature who was dear to him had gone with her. As soon as he was dressed for dinner he called Margaret on the telephone to know if she had arrived home safely, and was informed not only that she had, but that she was very wroth at him for getting her down three flights of stairs in the midst of her own dinner toilet.

"I had a kind of hunch, too," he told her, "and I felt as if I wanted to hear your voice speaking."

But she only scoffed at him.

"If that's the way you feel about your chauffeur," she said, "you ought to discharge him, but he brought me home beautifully."

The difference between a man's moments of prescience and a woman's, is that the man puts them out of his consciousness as quickly as he can, while a woman clings to them fearfully and goes her way a little more carefully for the momentary flash of foresight. David tried to see Margaret once or twice during that week but failed to find her in when he called or telephoned, and the special impulse to seek her alone again died naturally.

One Saturday a few weeks later Eleanor telegraphed him that she wished to come to New York for the week-end to do some shopping.

He went to the train to meet her, and when the slender chic figure in the most correct of tailor made suits appeared at the gateway, with an obsequious porter bearing her smart bag and ulster, he gave a sudden gasp of surprise at the picture. He had been aware for some time of the increase in her inches and the charm of the pure cameo-cut profile, but he regarded her still as a child histrionically assuming the airs and graces of womanhood, as small girl children masquerade in the trailing skirts of their elders. He was accustomed to the idea that she was growing up rapidly, but the fact that she was already grown had never actually dawned on him until this moment.

"You look as if you were surprised to see me, Uncle David,—are you?" she said, slipping a slim hand, warm through its immaculate glove, into his. "You knew I was coming, and you came to meet me, and yet you looked as surprised as if you hadn't expected me at all."

"Surprised to see you just about expresses it, Eleanor. I am surprised to see you. I was looking for a little girl in hair ribbons with her skirts to her knees."

"And a blue tam-o'-shanter?"

"And a blue tam-o'-shanter. I had forgotten you had grown up any to speak of."

"You see me every vacation," Eleanor grumbled, as she stepped into the waiting motor. "It isn't because you lack opportunity that you don't notice what I look like. It's just because you're naturally unobserving."

"Peter and Jimmie have been making a good deal of fuss about your being a young lady, now I think of it. Peter especially has been rather a nuisance about it, breaking into my most precious moments of triviality with the sweetly solemn thought that our little girl has grown to be a woman now."

"Oh, does *he* think I'm grown up, does he really?"

"Jimmie is almost as bad. He's all the time wanting me to get you to New York over the weekend, so that he can see if you are any taller than you were the last time he saw you."

"Are they coming to see me this evening?"

"Jimmie is going to look in. Peter is tied up with his sister. You know she's on here from China with her daughter. Peter wants you to meet the child."

"She must be as grown up as I am," Eleanor said. "I used to have her room, you know, when I stayed with Uncle Peter. Does Uncle Peter like her?"

"Not as much as he likes you, Miss Green-eyes. He says she looks like a heathen Chinee but otherwise is passable. I didn't know that you added jealousy to the list of your estimable vices."

"I'm not jealous," Eleanor protested; "or if I am it's only because she's blood relation,—and I'm not, you know."

"It's a good deal more prosaic to be a blood relation, if anybody should ask you," David smiled. "A blood relation is a good deal like the famous primrose on the river's brim."

"'A primrose by the river's brim a yellow primrose was to him,—and nothing more,'" Eleanor quoted gaily. "Why, what more—" she broke off suddenly and colored slightly.

"What more would anybody want to be than a yellow primrose by the river's brim?" David finished for her. "I don't know, I'm sure. I'm a mere man and such questions are too abstruse for me, as I told your Aunt Margaret the other day. Now I think of it, though, you don't look unlike a yellow primrose yourself to-day, daughter."

"That's because I've got a yellow ribbon on my hat."

"No, the resemblance goes much deeper. It has something to do with youth and fragrance and the flowers that bloom in the spring."

"The flowers that bloom in the spring, tra la," Eleanor returned saucily, "have nothing to do with the case."

"She's learning that she has eyes, good Lord," David said to himself, but aloud he remarked paternally, "I saw all your aunts yesterday. Gertrude gave a tea party and invited a great many famous tea party types, and ourselves."

"Was Aunt Beulah there?"

"I said all your aunts. Beulah was there, like the famous Queenie, with her hair in a braid."

"Not really."

"Pretty nearly. She's gone in for dress reform now, you know, a kind of middy blouse made out of a striped portière with a kilted skirt of the same material and a Scotch cap. She doesn't look so bad in it. Your Aunt Beulah presents a peculiar phenomenon these days. She's growing better-looking and behaving worse every day of her life."

"Behaving worse?"

"She's theory ridden and fad bitten. She'll come to a bad end if something doesn't stop her."

"Do you mean—stop her working for suffrage? I'm a suffragist, Uncle David."

"And quite right to remind me of it before I began slamming the cause. No, I don't mean suffrage. I believe in suffrage myself. I mean the way she's going after it. There are healthy ways of insisting on your rights and unhealthy ways. Beulah's getting further and further off key, that's all. Here we are at home, daughter. Your poor old cooperative father welcomes you to the associated hearthstone."

"This front entrance looks more like my front entrance than any other place does," Eleanor said. "Oh! I'm so glad to be here. George, how is the baby?" she asked the black elevator man, who beamed delightedly upon her.

"Gosh! I didn't know he had one," David chuckled. "It takes a woman—"

Jimmie appeared in the evening, laden with violets and a five pound box of the chocolates most in favor in the politest circles at the moment. David whistled when he saw them.

"What's devouring you, papa?" Jimmie asked him. "Don't I always place tributes at the feet of the offspring?"

"Mirror candy and street corner violets, yes," David said. "It's only the labels that surprised me."

"She knows the difference, now," Jimmie answered, "what would you?"

The night before her return to school it was decreed that she should go to bed early. She had spent two busy days of shopping and "seeing the family." She had her hours discussing her future with Peter, long visits and talks with Margaret and Gertrude, and a cup of tea at suffrage headquarters with Beulah, as well as long sessions in the shops accompanied by Mademoiselle, who made her home now permanently with David. She sat before the fire drowsily constructing pyramids out of the embers and David stood with one arm on the mantel, smoking his after-dinner cigar, and watching her.

"Is it to be college, Eleanor?" he asked her presently.

"I can't seem to make up my mind, Uncle David."

"Don't you like the idea?"

"Yes, I'd love it,—if—"

"If what, daughter?"

"If I thought I could spare the time."

"The time? Elucidate."

"I'm going to earn my own living, you know."

"I didn't know."

"I am. I've got to—in order to—to feel right about things."

"Don't you like the style of living to which your cooperative parents have accustomed you?"

"I love everything you've ever done for me, but I can't go on letting you do things for me forever."

"Why not?"

"I don't know why not exactly. It doesn't seem—right, that's all."

"It's your New England conscience, Eleanor; one of the most specious varieties of consciences in the world. It will always be tempting you to do good that better may come. Don't listen to it, daughter."

"I'm in earnest, Uncle David. I don't know whether I would be better fitted to earn my living if I went to business college or real college. What do you think?"

"I can't think,—I'm stupefied."

"Uncle Peter couldn't think, either."

"Have you mentioned this brilliant idea to Peter?"

"Yes."

"What did he say?"

"He talked it over with me, but I think he thinks I'll change my mind."

"I think you'll change your mind. Good heavens! Eleanor, we're all able to afford you—the little we spend on you is nothing divided among six of us. It's our pleasure and privilege. When did you come to this extraordinary decision?"

"A long time ago. The day that Mrs. Bolling talked to me, I think. There are things she said that I've never forgotten. I told Uncle Peter to think about it and then help me to decide which to do, and I want you to think, Uncle David, and tell me truly what you believe the best preparation for a business life would be. I thought perhaps I might be a stenographer in an editorial office, and my training there would be more use to me than four years at college, but I don't know."

"You're an extraordinary young woman," David said, staring at her. "I'm glad you broached this subject, if only that I might realize how extraordinary, but I don't think anything will come of it, my dear. I don't want you to go to college unless you really want to, but if you do want to, I hope you will take up the pursuit of learning as a pursuit and not as a means to an end. Do you hear me, daughter?"

"Yes, Uncle David."

"Then let's have no more of this nonsense of earning your own living."

"Are you really displeased, Uncle David?"

"I should be if I thought you were serious,—but it's bedtime. If you're going to get your beauty sleep, my dear, you ought to begin on it immediately."

Eleanor rose obediently, her brow clouded a little, and her head held high. David watched the color coming and going in the sweet face and the tender breast rising and falling with her quickening breath.

"I thought perhaps you would understand," she said. "Good night."

She had always kissed him "good night" until this visit, and he had refrained from commenting on the omission before, but now he put out his hand to her.

"Haven't you forgotten something?" he asked. "There is only one way for a daughter to say good night to her parent."

She put up her face, and as she did so he caught the glint of tears in her eyes.

"Why, Eleanor, dear," he said, "did you care?" And he kissed her. Then his lips sought hers again.

With his arms still about her shoulder he stood looking down at her. A hot tide of crimson made its way slowly to her brow and then receded, accentuating the clear pallor of her face.

"That was a real kiss, dear," he said slowly. "We mustn't get such things confused. I won't bother you with talking about it to-night, or until you are ready. Until then we'll pretend that it didn't happen, but if the thought of it should ever disturb you the least bit, dear, you are to remember that the time is coming when I shall have something to say about it; will you remember?"

"Yes, Uncle David," Eleanor said uncertainly, "but I—I—"

David took her unceremoniously by the shoulders.

"Go now," he said, and she obeyed him without further question.

CHAPTER XVIII

BEULAH'S PROBLEM

Peter was shaving for the evening. His sister was giving a dinner party for two of her husband's fellow bankers and their wives. After that they were going to see the latest Belasco production, and from there to some one of the new dancing "clubs,"—the smart cabarets that were forced to organize in the guise of private enterprises to evade the two o'clock closing law. Peter enjoyed dancing, but he did not as a usual thing enjoy bankers' wives. He was deliberating on the possibility of excusing himself gracefully after the theater, on the plea of having some work to do, and finally decided that his sister's feelings would be hurt if she realized he was trying to escape the climax of the hospitality she had provided so carefully.

He gazed at himself intently over the drifts of lather and twisted his shaving mirror to the most propitious angle from time to time. In the room across the hall—Eleanor's room, he always called it to himself—his young niece was singing bits of the Mascagni intermezzo interspersed with bits of the latest musical comedy, in a rather uncertain contralto.

"My last girl came from Vassar, and I don't know where to class her."

Peter's mind took up the refrain automatically. "My last girl—" and began at the beginning of the chorus again. "My last girl came from Vassar," which brought him by natural stages to the consideration of the higher education and of Beulah, and a conversation concerning her that he had had with Jimmie and David the night before.

"She's off her nut," Jimmie said succinctly. "It's not exactly that there's nobody home," he rapped his curly pate significantly, "but there's too much of a crowd there. She's not the same old girl at all. She used to be a good fellow, high-brow propaganda and all. Now she's got nothing else in her head. What's happened to her?"

"It's what hasn't happened to her that's addled her," David explained. "It's these highly charged, hypersensitive young women that go to pieces under the modern pressure. They're the ones that need licking into shape by all the natural processes."

"By which you mean a drunken husband and a howling family?" Jimmie suggested.

"Yes, or its polite equivalent."

"That is true, isn't it?" Peter said. "Feminism isn't the answer to Beulah's problem."

"It is the problem," David said; "she's poisoning herself with it. I know what I'm talking about. I've seen it happen. My cousin Jack married a girl with a sister a great deal like Beulah, looks, temperament, and everything else, though she wasn't half so nice. She got going the militant pace and couldn't stop herself. I never met her at a dinner party that she wasn't tackling somebody on the subject of man's inhumanity to woman. She ended in a sanitorium; in fact, they're thinking now of taking her to the—"

"—bug house," Jimmie finished cheerfully.

"And in the beginning she was a perfectly good girl that needed nothing in the world but a chance to develop along legitimate lines."

"The frustrate matron, eh?" Peter said.

"The frustrate matron," David agreed gravely. "I wonder you haven't realized this yourself, Gram. You're keener about such things than I am. Beulah is more your job than mine."

"Is she?"

"You're the only one she listens to or looks up to. Go up and tackle her some day and see what you can do. She's sinking fast."

"Give her the once over and throw out the lifeline," Jimmie said.

"I thought all this stuff was a phase, a part of her taking herself seriously as she always has. I had no idea it was anything to worry about," Peter persisted. "Are you sure she's in bad shape—that she's got anything more than a bad attack of Feminism of the Species in its most virulent form? They come out of *that*, you know."

"She's batty," Jimmie nodded gravely. "Dave's got the right dope."

"Go up and look her over," David persisted; "you'll see what we mean, then. Beulah's in a bad way."

Peter reviewed this conversation while he shaved the right side of his face, and frowned prodigiously through the lather. He wished that he had an engagement that evening that he could break in order to get to see Beulah at once, and discover for himself the harm that had come to his friend. He was devoted to Beulah. He had always felt that he saw a little more clearly than the others the virtue that was in the girl. He admired the pluck with which she made her attack on life and the energy with which she accomplished her ends. There was to him something alluring and quaint about her earnestness. The fact that her soundness could be questioned came to him with something like a shock. As soon as he was dressed he was called to the telephone to talk to David.

"Margaret has just told me that Doctor Penrose has been up to see Beulah and pronounces it a case of nervous breakdown. He wants her to try out psycho-analysis, and that sort of thing. He seems to feel that it's serious. Margaret is fearfully upset, poor girl. So'm I, to tell the truth."

"And so am I," Peter acknowledged to himself as he hung up the receiver. He was so absorbed during the evening that one of the ladies—the wife of the fat banker—found him extremely dull and decided against asking him to dinner with his sister. The wife of the thin banker, who was in his charge at the theater, got the benefit of his effort to rouse himself and grace the occasion creditably, and found him delightful. By the time the evening was over he had decided that Beulah should be pulled out of whatever dim world of dismay and delusion she might be wandering in, at whatever cost. It was unthinkable that she should be wasted, or that her youth and splendid vitality should go for naught.

He found her eager to talk to him the next night when he went to see her.

"Peter," she said, "I want you to go to my aunt and my mother, and tell them that I've got to go on with my work,—that I can't be stopped and interrupted by this foolishness of doctors and nurses. I never felt better in my life, except for not being able to sleep, and I think that is due to the way they have worried me. I live in a world they don't know anything about, that's all. Even if they were right, if I am wearing myself out soul and body for the sake of the cause, what business is it of theirs to interfere? I'm working for the souls and bodies of women for ages to come. What difference does it make if my soul and body suffer? Why shouldn't they?" Her eyes narrowed. Peter observed the unnatural light in them, the apparent dryness of her lips, the two bright spots burning below her cheek-bones.

"Because," he answered her slowly, "I don't think it was the original intention of Him who put us here that we should sacrifice everything we are to the business of emphasizing the superiority of a sex."

"That isn't the point at all, Peter. No man understands, no man can understand. It's woman's equality we want emphasized, just literally that and nothing more. You've pauperized and degraded us long enough—"

"Thou canst not say I—" Peter began.

"Yes, you and every other man, every man in the world is a party to it."

"I had to get her going," Peter apologized to himself, "in order to get a point of departure. Not if I vote for women, Beulah, dear," he added aloud.

"If you throw your influence with us instead of against us," she conceded, "you're helping to right the wrong that you have permitted for so long."

"Well, granting your premise, granting all your premises, Beulah—and I admit that most of them have sound reasoning behind them—your battle now is all over but the shouting. There's no reason that you personally should sacrifice your last drop of energy to a campaign that's practically won already."

"If you think the mere franchise is all I have been working for, Peter,—"

"I don't. I know the thousand and one activities you women are concerned with. I know how much better church and state always have been and are bound to be, when the women get behind and push, if they throw their strength right."

Beulah rose enthusiastically to this bait and talked rationally and well for some time. Just as Peter was beginning to feel that David and Jimmie had been guilty of the most unsympathetic exaggeration of her state of mind—unquestionably she was not as fit physically as usual—she startled him with an abrupt change into almost hysterical incoherence.

"I have a right to live my own life," she concluded, "and nobody—nobody shall stop me."

"We are all living our own lives, aren't we?" Peter asked mildly.

"No woman lives her own life to-day," Beulah cried, still excitedly. "Every woman is living the life of some man, who has the legal right to treat her as an imbecile."

"Hold on, Beulah. How about the suffrage states, how about the women who are already in the proud possession of their rights and privileges? They are not technical imbeciles any longer according to your theory. The vote's coming. Every woman will be a super-woman in two shakes,—so what's devouring you, as Jimmie says?"

"It's after all the states have suffrage that the big fight will really begin," Beulah answered wearily. "It's the habit of wearing the yoke we'll have to fight then."

"The anti-feminists," Peter said, "I see. Beulah, can't you give yourself any rest, or is the nature of the cause actually suicidal?"

To his surprise her tense face quivered at this and she tried to steady a tremulous lower lip.

"I am tired," she said, a little piteously, "dreadfully tired, but nobody cares."

"Is that fair?"

"It's true."

"Your friends care."

"They only want to stop me doing something they have no sympathy with. What do Gertrude and Margaret know of the real purpose of my life or my failure or success? They take a sentimental interest in my health, that's all. Do you suppose it made any difference to Jeanne d'Arc how many people took a sympathetic interest in her health if they didn't believe in what she believed in?"

"There's something in that."

"I thought Eleanor would grow up to take an interest in the position of women, and to care about the things I cared about, but she's not going to."

"She's very fond of you."

"Not as fond as she is of Margaret."

Peter longed to dispute this, but he could not in honesty.

"She's a suffragist."

"She's so lukewarm she might just as well be an anti. She's naturally reactionary. Women like that aren't much use. They drag us back like so much dead weight."

"I suppose Eleanor has been a disappointment to you," Peter mused, "but she tries pretty hard to be all things to all parents, Beulah. You'll find she won't fail you if you need her."

"I shan't need her," Beulah said, prophetically. "I hoped she'd stand beside me in the work, but she's not that kind. She'll marry early and have a family, and that will be the end of her."

"I wonder if she will," Peter said, "I hope so. She still seems such a child to me. I believe in marriage, Beulah, don't you?"

Her answer surprised him.

"Under certain conditions, I do. I made a vow once that I would never marry and I've always believed that it would be hampering and limiting to a woman, but now I see that the fight has got to go on. If there are going to be women to carry on the fight they will have to be born of the women who are fighting to-day."

"Thank God," Peter said devoutly. "It doesn't make any difference why you believe it, if you do believe it."

"It makes all the difference," Beulah said, but her voice softened. "What I believe is more to me than anything else in the world, Peter."

"That's all right, too. I understand your point of view, Beulah. You carry it a little bit too far, that's all that's wrong with it from my way of thinking."

"Will you help me to go on, Peter?"

"How?"

"Talk to my aunt and my mother. Tell them that they're all wrong in their treatment of me."

"I think I could undertake to do that"—Peter was convinced that a less antagonistic attitude on the part of her relatives would be more successful—"and I will."

Beulah's eyes filled with tears.

"You're the only one who comes anywhere near knowing," she said, "or who ever will, I guess. I try so hard, Peter, and now when I don't seem to be accomplishing as much as I want to, as much as it's necessary for me to accomplish if I am to go on respecting myself, every one enters into a conspiracy to stop my doing anything at all. The only thing that makes me nervous is the way I am thwarted and opposed at every turn. I haven't got nervous prostration."

"Perhaps not, but you have something remarkably like *ideê fixe*," Peter said to himself compassionately.

He found her actual condition less dangerous but much more difficult than he had anticipated. She was living wrong, that was the sum and substance of her malady. Her life was spent confronting theories and discounting conditions. She did not realize that it is only the interest of our investment in life that we can sanely contribute to the cause of living. Our capital strength and energy must be used for the struggle for existence itself if we are to have a world of balanced individuals. There is an arrogance involved in assuming ourselves more humane than human that reacts insidiously on our health and morals. Peter, looking into the twitching hectic face before him with the telltale glint of mania in the eyes, felt himself becoming helpless with pity for a mind gone so far askew. He felt curiously responsible for Beulah's condition.

"She wouldn't have run herself so far aground," he thought, "if I had been on the job a little more. I could have helped her to steer straighter. A word here and a lift there and she would have come through all right. Now something's got to stop her or she can't be stopped. She'll preach once too often out of the tail of a cart on the subject of equal guardianship,—and—"

Beulah put her hands to her face suddenly, and, sinking back into the depths of the big cushioned chair on the edge of which she had been tensely poised during most of the conversation, burst into tears.

"You're the only one that knows," she sobbed over and over again. "I'm so tired, Peter, but I've got to go on and on and on. If they stop me, I'll kill myself."

Peter crossed the room to her side and sat down on her chair-arm.

"Don't cry, dear," he said, with a hand on her head. "You're too tired to think things out now,—but I'll help you."

She lifted a piteous face, for the moment so startlingly like that of the dead girl he had loved that his senses were confused by the resemblance.

"How, Peter?" she asked. "How can you help me?"

"I think I see the way," he said slowly.

He slipped to his knees and gathered her close in his arms.

"I think this will be the way, dear," he said very gently.

"Does this mean that you want me to marry you?" she whispered, when she was calmer.

"If you will, dear," he said. "Will you?"

"I will,—if I can, if I can make it seem right to after I've thought it all out.— Oh! Peter, I love you. I love you."

"I had no idea of that," he said gravely, "but it's wonderful that you do. I'll put everything I've got into trying to make you happy, Beulah."

"I know you will, Peter." Her arms closed around his neck and tightened there. "I love you."

He made her comfortable and she relaxed like a tired child, almost asleep under his soothing hand, and the quiet spell of his tenderness.

"I didn't know it could be like this," she whispered.

"But it can," he answered her.

In his heart he was saying, "This is best. I am sure this is best. It is the right and normal way for her—and for me."

In her tri-cornered dormitory room at the new school which she was not sharing with any one this year Eleanor, enveloped in a big brown and yellow wadded bathrobe, was writing a letter to Peter. Her hair hung in two golden brown braids over her shoulders and her pure profile was bent intently over the paper. At the moment when Beulah made her confession of love and closed her eyes against the breast of the man who had just asked her to marry him, two big tears forced their way between Eleanor's lids and splashed down upon her letter.

CHAPTER XIX

Mostly Uncle Peter

"Dear Uncle Peter," the letter ran, "I am very, very homesick and lonely for you to-day. It seems to me that I would gladly give a whole year of my life just for the privilege of being with you, and talking instead of writing,—but since that can not be, I am going to try and write you about the thing that is troubling me. I can't bear it alone any longer, and still I don't know whether it is the kind of thing that it is honorable to tell or not. So you see I am very much troubled and puzzled, and this trouble involves some one else in a way that it is terrible to think of.

"Uncle Peter, dear, I do not want to be married. Not until I have grown up, and seen something of the world. You know it is one of my dearest wishes to be self-supporting, not because I am a Feminist or a new woman, or have 'the unnatural belief of an antipathy to man' that you're always talking about, but just because it will prove to me once and for all that I belong to myself, and that my *soul* isn't, and never has been cooperative. You know what I mean by this, and you are not hurt by my feeling so. You, I am sure, would not want me to be married, or to have to think of myself as engaged, especially not to anybody that we all knew and loved, and who is very close to me and you in quite another way. Please don't try to imagine what I mean, Uncle Peter—even if you know, you must tell yourself that you don't know. Please, please pretend even to yourself that I haven't written you this letter. I know people do tell things like this, but I don't know quite how they bring themselves to do it, even if they have somebody like you who understands everything—everything.

"Uncle Peter, dear, I am supposed to be going to be married by and by when the one who wants it feels that it can be spoken of, and until that happens, I've got to wait for him to speak, unless I can find some way to tell him that I do not want it ever to be. I don't know how to tell him. I don't know how to make him feel that I do not belong to him. It is only myself I belong to, and I belong to you, but I don't know how to make that plain to any one who does not know it already. I can't say it unless perhaps you can help me to.

"I am different from the other girls. I know every girl always thinks there is something different about her, but I think there are ways in which I truly am different. When I want anything I know more clearly what it is, and why I want it than most other girls do, and not only that, but I know now, that I want to keep myself, and everything I think and feel and am,—*sacred*. There is an inner shrine in a woman's soul that she must keep inviolate. I know that now.

"A liberty that you haven't known how, or had the strength to prevent, is a terrible thing. One can't forget it. Uncle Peter, dear, twice in my life things have happened that drive me almost desperate when I think of them. If these things should happen again when I know that I don't want them to, I don't think there would be any way of my bearing it. Perhaps you can tell me something that will make me find a way out of this tangle. I don't see what it could be, but lots of times you have shown me the way out of endless mazes that were not grown up troubles like this, but seemed very real to me just the same.

"Uncle Peter, dear, dear, dear,—you are all I have. I wish you were here to-night, though you wouldn't be let in, even if you beat on the gate ever so hard, for it's long after bedtime. I am up in my tower room all alone. Oh! answer this letter. Answer it quickly, quickly."

Eleanor read her letter over and addressed a tear splotched envelope to Peter. Then she slowly tore letter and envelope into little bits.

"He would know," she said to herself. "I haven't any real right to tell him. It would be just as bad as any kind of tattling."

She began another letter to him but found she could not write without saying what was in her heart, and so went to bed uncomforted. There was nothing in her experience to help her in her relation to David. His kiss on her lips had taught her the nature of such kisses: had made her understand suddenly the ease with which the strange, sweet spell of sex is cast. She related it to the episode of the unwelcome caress bestowed upon her by the brother of Maggie Lou, and that half forgotten incident took on an almost terrible significance. She understood now how she should have repelled that unconscionable boy, but that understanding did not help her with the problem of her Uncle David. Though the thought of it thrilled through her with a strange incredible delight, she did not want another kiss of his upon her lips.

"It's—it's—like that," she said to herself. "I want it to be from somebody—else. Somebody *realer* to me. Somebody that would make it seem right." But even to herself she mentioned no names.

She had definitely decided against going to college. She felt that she must get upon her own feet quickly and be under no obligation to any man. Vaguely her stern New England rearing was beginning to indicate the way that she should tread. No man or woman who did not understand "the value of a dollar," was properly equipped to do battle with the realities of life. The value of a dollar, and a clear title to it—these were the principles upon which her integrity must be founded if she were to survive her own self-respect. Her

Puritan fathers had bestowed this heritage upon her. She had always felt the irregularity of her economic position; now that the complication of her relation with David had arisen, it was beginning to make her truly uncomfortable.

David had been very considerate of her, but his consideration frightened her. He had been so afraid that she might be hurt or troubled by his attitude toward her that he had explained again, and almost in so many words that he was only waiting for her to grow accustomed to the idea before he asked her to become his wife. She had looked forward with considerable trepidation to the Easter vacation following the establishment of their one-sided understanding, but David relieved her apprehension by putting up at his club and leaving her in undisturbed possession of his quarters. There, with Mademoiselle still treating her as a little girl, and the other five of her heterogeneous foster family to pet and divert her at intervals, she soon began to feel her life swing back into a more accustomed and normal perspective. David's attitude to her was as simple as ever, and when she was with the devoted sextet she was almost able to forget the matter that was at issue between them—almost but not quite.

She took quite a new kind of delight in her association with the group. She found herself suddenly on terms of grown up equality with them. Her consciousness of the fact that David was tacitly waiting for her to become a woman, had made a woman of her already, and she looked on her guardians with the eyes of a woman, even though a very newly fledged and timorous one.

She was a trifle self-conscious with the others, but with Jimmie she was soon on her old familiar footing.

"Uncle Jimmie is still a great deal of fun," she wrote in her diary. "He does just the same old things he used to do with me, and a good many new ones in addition. He brings me flowers, and gets me taxi-cabs as if I were really a grown up young lady, and he pinches my nose and teases me as if I were still the little girl that kept house in a studio for him. I never realized before what a good-looking man he is. I used to think that Uncle Peter was the only handsome man of the three, but now I realize that they are all exceptionally good-looking. Uncle David has a great deal of distinction, of course, but Uncle Jimmie is merry and radiant and vital, and tall and athletic looking into the bargain. The ladies on the Avenue all turn to look at him when we go walking. He says that the gentlemen all turn to look at me, and I think perhaps they do when I have my best clothes on, but in my school clothes I am quite certain that nothing like that happens.

"I have been out with Uncle Jimmie Tuesday and Wednesday and Thursday and Friday,—four days of my vacation. We've been to the Hippodrome and Chinatown, and we've dined at Sherry's, and one night we went down to the little Italian restaurant where I had my first introduction to *eau rougie*, and was so distressed about it. I shall never forget that night, and I don't think Uncle Jimmie will ever be done teasing me about it. It is nice to be with Uncle Jimmie so much, but I never seem to see Uncle Peter any more. Alphonse is very careful about taking messages, I know, but it does seem to me that Uncle Peter must have telephoned more times than I know of. It does seem as if he would, at least, try to see me long enough to have one of our old time talks again. To see him with all the others about is only a very little better than not seeing him at all. He isn't like himself, someway. There is a shadow over him that I do not understand."

"Don't you think that Uncle Peter has changed?" she asked Jimmie, when the need of speaking of him became too strong to withstand.

"He is a little pale about the ears," Jimmie conceded, "but I think that's the result of hard work and not enough exercise. He spends all his spare time trying to patch up Beulah instead of tramping and getting out on his horse the way he used to. He's doing a good job on the old dear, but it's some job, nevertheless and notwithstanding—"

"Is Aunt Beulah feeling better than she was?" Eleanor's lips were dry, but she did her best to make her voice sound natural. It seemed strange that Jimmie could speak so casually of a condition of affairs that made her very heart stand still. "I didn't know that Uncle Peter had been taking care of her."

"Taking care of her isn't a circumstance to what Peter has been doing for Beulah. You know she hasn't been right for some time. She got burning wrong, like the flame on our old gas stove in the studio when there was air in it."

"Uncle David thought so the last time I was here," Eleanor said, "but I didn't know that Uncle Peter—"

"Peter, curiously enough, was the last one to tumble. Dave and I got alarmed about the girl and held a consultation, with the result that Doctor Gramercy was called. If we'd believed he would go into it quite so heavily we might have thought again before we sicked him on. It's very nice for Mary Ann, but rather tough on Abraham as they said when the lady was deposited on that already overcrowded bosom. Now Beulah's got suffrage mania, and Peter's got Beulah mania, and it's a merry mess all around."

"Is Uncle Peter with her a lot?"

"Every minute. You haven't seen much of him since you came, have you?—Well, the reason is that every afternoon as soon as he can get away from the office, he puts on a broad sash marked 'Votes for Women,' and trundles Beulah around in her little white and green perambulator, trying to distract her mind from suffrage while he talks to her gently and persuasively upon the subject. Suffrage is the only subject on her mind, he explains, so all he can do is to try to cuckoo gently under it day by day. It's a very complicated process but he's making headway."

"I'm glad of that," Eleanor said faintly. "How—how is Aunt Gertrude? I don't see her very often, either."

"Gertrude's all right." It was Jimmie's turn to look self-conscious. "She never has time for me any more; I'm not high-brow enough for her. She's getting on like a streak, you know, exhibiting everywhere."

"I know she is. She gave me a cast of her faun's head. I think it is lovely. Aunt Margaret looks well."

"She is, I guess, but don't let's waste all our valuable time talking about the family. Let's talk about us—you and me. You ask me how I'm feeling and then I'll tell you. Then I'll ask you how you're feeling and you'll tell me. Then I'll tell you how I imagine you must be feeling from the way you're looking,—and that will give me a chance to expatiate on the delectability of your appearance. I'll work up delicately to the point where you will begin to compare me favorably with all the other nice young men you know,—and then we'll be off."

"Shall we?" Eleanor asked, beginning to sparkle a little.

"We shall indeed," he assured her solemnly. "You begin. No, on second thoughts, I'll begin. I'll begin at the place where I start telling you how excessively well you're looking. I don't know, considering its source, whether it would interest you or not, but you have the biggest blue eyes that I've, ever seen in all my life,—and I'm rather a judge of them."

"All the better to eat you with, my dear," Eleanor chanted.

"Quite correct." He shot her a queer glance from under his eyebrows. "I don't feel very safe when I look into them, my child. It would be a funny joke on me if they did prove fatal to me, wouldn't it?—well,—but away with such nonsense. I mustn't blither to the very babe whose cradle I am rocking, must I?"

"I'm not a babe, Uncle Jimmie. I feel very old sometimes. Older than any of you."

"Oh! you are, you are. You're a regular sphinx sometimes. Peter says that you even disconcert him at times, when you take to remembering things out of your previous experience."

"'When he was a King in Babylon and I was a Christian Slave?'" she quoted quickly.

"Exactly. Only I'd prefer to play the part of the King of Babylon, if it's all the same to you, niecelet. How does the rest of it go, 'yet not for a—' something or other 'would I wish undone that deed beyond the grave.' Gosh, my dear, if things were otherwise, I think I could understand how that feller felt. Get on your hat, and let's get out into the open. My soul is cramped with big potentialities this afternoon. I wish you hadn't grown up, Eleanor. You are taking my breath away in a peculiar manner. No man likes to have his breath taken away so suddint like. Let's get out into the rolling prairie of Central Park."

But the rest of the afternoon was rather a failure. The Park had that peculiar bleakness that foreruns the first promise of spring. The children, that six weeks before were playing in the snow and six weeks later would be searching the turf for dandelions, were in the listless between seasons state of comparative inactivity. There was a deceptive balminess in the air that seemed merely to overlay a penetrating chilliness.

"I'm sorry I'm not more entertaining this afternoon," Jimmie apologized on the way home. "It isn't that I am not happy, or that I don't feel the occasion to be more than ordinarily propitious; I'm silent upon a peak in Darien,— that's all."

"I was thinking of something else, too," Eleanor said.

"I didn't say I was thinking of something else."

"People are always thinking of something else when they aren't talking to each other, aren't they?"

"Something else, or each other, Eleanor. I wasn't thinking of something else, I was thinking—well, I won't tell you exactly—at present. A penny for your thoughts, little one."

"They aren't worth it."

"A penny is a good deal of money. You can buy joy for a penny."

"I'm afraid I couldn't—buy joy, even if you gave me your penny, Uncle Jimmie."

"You might try. My penny might not be like other pennies. On the other hand, your thoughts might be worth a fortune to me."

"I'm afraid they wouldn't be worth anything to anybody."

"You simply don't know what I am capable of making out of them."

"I wish I could make something out of them," Eleanor said so miserably that Jimmie was filled with compunction for having tired her out, and hailed a passing taxi in which to whiz her home again.

"I have found out that Uncle Peter is spending all his time with Aunt Beulah," she wrote in her diary that evening. "It is beautiful of him to try to help her through this period of nervous collapse, and just like him, but I don't understand why it is that he doesn't come and tell me about it, especially since he is getting so tired. He ought to know that I love him so dearly and deeply that I could help him even in helping her. It isn't like him not to share his anxieties with me. Aunt Beulah is a grown up woman, and has friends and doctors and nurses, and every one knows her need. It seems to me that he might think that I have no one but him, and that whatever might lie heavy on my heart I could only confide in him. I have always told him everything. Why doesn't it occur to him that I might have something to tell him now? Why doesn't he come to me?

"I am afraid he will get sick. He needs a good deal of exercise to keep in form. If he doesn't have a certain amount of muscular activity his digestion is not so good. There are two little creases between his eyes that I never remember seeing there before. I asked him the other night when he was here with Aunt Beulah if his head ached, and he said 'no,' but Aunt Beulah said her head ached almost all the time. Of course, Aunt Beulah is important, and if Uncle Peter is trying to bring her back to normality again she is important to him, and that makes her important to me for his sake also, but nobody in the world is worth the sacrifice of Uncle Peter. Nobody, nobody.

"I suppose it's a part of his great beauty that he should think so disparagingly of himself. I might not love him so well if he knew just how dear and sweet and great his personality is. It isn't so much what he says or does, or even the way he looks that constitutes his charm, it's the simple power and radiance behind his slightest move. Oh! I can't express it. He doesn't think he is especially fine or beautiful. He doesn't know what a waste it is when he spends his strength upon somebody who isn't as noble in character as he is,—but I know, and it makes me wild to think of it. Oh! why doesn't he come to me? My vacation is almost over, and I don't see how I could bear going back to school without one comforting hour of him alone.

"I intended to write a detailed account of my vacation, but I can not. Uncle Jimmie has certainly tried to make me happy. He is so funny and dear. I could have so much fun with him if I were not worried about Uncle Peter!

"Uncle David says he wants to spend my last evening with me. We are going to dine here, and then go to the theater together. I am going to try to tell him how I feel about things, but I am afraid he won't give me the chance. Life is a strange mixture of things you want and can't have, and things you can have and don't want. It seems almost disloyal to put that down on paper about Uncle David. I do want him and love him, but oh!—not in that way. Not in that way. There is only one person in a woman's life that she can feel that way about. Why—why—why doesn't my Uncle Peter come to me?"

CHAPTER XX

"Just by way of formality," David said, "and not because I think any one present"—he smiled on the five friends grouped about his dinner table—"still takes our old resolution seriously, I should like to be released from the anti-matrimonial pledge that I signed eight years ago this November. I have no announcement to make as yet, but when I do wish to make an announcement—and I trust to have the permission granted very shortly—I want to be sure of my technical right to do so."

"Gosh all Hemlocks!" Jimmie exclaimed in a tone of such genuine confusion that it raised a shout of laughter. "I never thought of that."

"Nor I," said Peter. "I never signed any pledge to that effect."

"We left you out of it, Old Horse, regarding you as a congenital celibate anyway," Jimmie answered.

"Some day soon you will understand how much you wronged me," Peter said with a covert glance at Beulah.

"I wish I could say as much," Jimmie sighed, "since this is the hour of confession I don't mind adding that I hope I may be able to soon."

Gertrude clapped her hands softly.

"Wonderful, wonderful!" she cried. "We've the makings of a triple wedding in our midst. Look into the blushing faces before us and hear the voice that breathed o'er Eden echoing in our ears. This is the most exciting moment of my life! Girls, get on your feet and drink to the health of these about-to-be Benedicts. Up in your chairs,—one slipper on the table. Now!"—and the moment was saved.

Gertrude had seen Margaret's sudden pallor and heard the convulsive catching of her breath,—Margaret rising Undine-like out of a filmy, pale green frock, with her eyes set a little more deeply in the shadows than usual. Her quick instinct to the rescue was her own salvation.

David was on his feet.

"On behalf of my coadjutors," he said, "I thank you. All this is extremely premature for me, and I imagine from the confusion of the other gentlemen present it is as much, if not more so, for them. Personally I regret exceedingly being unable to take you more fully into my confidence. The only reason for this partial revelation is that I wished to be sure that I was honorably released from my oath of abstinence. Hang it all! You fellows say something," he concluded, sinking abruptly into his chair.

"Your style always was distinctly mid-Victorian," Jimmie murmured. "I've got nothing to say, except that I wish I had something to say and that if I *do* have something to say in the near future I'll create a real sensation! When Miss Van Astorbilt permits David to link her name with his in the caption under a double column cut in our leading journals, you'll get nothing like the thrill that I expect to create with my modest announcement. I've got a real romance up my sleeve."

"So've I, Jimmie. There is no Van Astorbilt in mine."

"Some simple bar-maid then? A misalliance in our midst. Now about you, Peter?"

"The lady won't give me her permission to speak," Peter said. "She knows how proud and happy I shall be when I am able to do so."

Beulah looked up suddenly.

"It is better we should marry," she said. "I didn't realize that when I exacted that oath from you. It is from the intellectual type that the brains to carry on the great work of the world must be inherited."

"I pass," Jimmie murmured. "Where's the document we signed?"

"I've got it. I'll destroy it to-night and then we may all consider ourselves free to take any step that we see fit. It was really only as a further protection to Eleanor that we signed it."

"Eleanor will be surprised, won't she?" Gertrude suggested. Three self-conscious masculine faces met her innocent interrogation.

"*Eleanor*," Margaret breathed, "*Eleanor*."

"I rather think she will," Jimmie chuckled irresistibly, but David said nothing, and Peter stared unseeingly into the glass he was still twirling on its stem.

"Eleanor will be taken care of just the same," Beulah said decisively. "I don't think we need even go through the formality of a vote on that."

"Eleanor will be taken care of," David said softly.

The Hutchinsons' limousine—old Grandmother Hutchinson had a motor nowadays—was calling for Margaret, and she was to take the two other girls home. David and Jimmie—such is the nature of men—were disappointed in not being able to take Margaret and Gertrude respectively under their accustomed protection.

"I wanted to talk to you, Gertrude," Jimmie said reproachfully as she slipped away from his ingratiating hand on her arm.

"I thought I should take you home to-night, Margaret," David said; "you never gave me the slip before."

"The old order changeth," Gertrude replied lightly to them both, as she preceded Margaret into the luxurious interior.

"It's Eleanor," Gertrude announced as the big car swung into Fifth Avenue.

"Which is Eleanor?" Margaret cried hysterically.

"What do you mean?" Beulah asked.

"Jimmie or David—or—or both are going to marry Eleanor. Didn't you see their faces when Beulah spoke of her?"

"David wants to marry Eleanor," Margaret said quietly. "I've known it all winter—without realizing what it was I knew."

"Well, who is Jimmy going to marry then?" Beulah inquired.

"Who is Peter going to marry for that matter?" Gertrude cut in. "Oh! it doesn't make any difference,—we're losing them just the same."

"Not necessarily," Beulah said. "No matter what combinations come about, we shall still have an indestructible friendship."

"Indestructible friendship—shucks," Gertrude cried. "The boys are going to be married—married—married! Marriage is the one thing that indestructible friendships don't survive—except as ghosts."

"It should be Peter who is going to marry Eleanor," Margaret said. "It's Peter who has always loved her best. It's Peter she cares for."

"As a friend," Beulah said, "as her dearest friend."

"Not as a friend," Margaret answered softly, "she loves him. She has always loved him. It comes early sometimes."

"I don't believe it. I simply don't believe it."

"I believe it," Gertrude said. "I hadn't thought of it before. Of course, it must be Peter who is going to marry her."

"If it isn't we've succeeded in working out a rather tragic experiment," Margaret said, "haven't we?"

"Life is a tragic experiment for any woman," Gertrude said sententiously.

"Peter doesn't intend to marry Eleanor," Beulah persisted. "I happen to know."

"Do you happen to know who he is going to marry?"

"Yes, I do know, but I—I can't tell you yet."

"Whoever it is, it's a mistake," Margaret said. "It's our little Eleanor he wants. I suppose he doesn't realize it himself yet, and when he does it will be too late. He's probably gone and tied himself up with somebody entirely unsuitable, hasn't he, Beulah?"

"I don't know," Beulah said; "perhaps he has. I hadn't thought of it that way."

"It's the way to think of it, I know." Margaret's eyes filled with sudden tears. "But whatever he's done it's past mending now. There'll be no question of Peter's backing out of a bargain—bad or good, and our poor little kiddie's got to suffer."

"Beulah took it hard," Gertrude commented, as they turned up-town again after dropping their friend at her door. The two girls were spending the night together at Margaret's. "I wonder on what grounds. I think besides being devoted to Eleanor, she feels terrifically responsible for her. She isn't quite herself again either."

"She is almost, thanks to Peter."

"But—oh! I can't pretend to think of anything else,—who—who—who—are our boys going to marry?"

"I don't know, Gertrude."

"But you care?"

"It's a blow."

"I always thought that you and David—"

Margaret met her eyes bravely but she did not answer the implicit question.

"I always thought that you and Jimmie—" she said presently. "Oh! Gertrude, you would have been so good for him."

"Oh! it's all over now," Gertrude said, "but I didn't know that a living soul suspected me."

"I've known for a long time."

"Are you really hurt, dear?" Gertrude whispered as they clung to each other.

"Not really. It could have been—that's all. He could have made me care. I've never seen any one else whom I thought that of. I—I was so used to him."

"That's the rub," Gertrude said, "we're so used to them. They're so—so preposterously necessary to us."

Late that night clasped in each other's arms they admitted the extent of their desolation. Life had been robbed of a magic,—a mystery. The solid friendship of years of mutual trust and understanding was the background of so much lovely folly, so many unrealized possibilities, so many nebulous desires and dreams that the sudden dissolution of their circle was an unthinkable calamity.

"We ought to have put out our hands and taken them if we wanted them," Gertrude said, out of the darkness. "Other women do. Probably these other women have. Men are helpless creatures. They need to be firmly turned in the right direction instead of being given their heads. We've been too good to our boys. We ought to have snitched them."

"I wouldn't pay that price for love," Margaret said. "I couldn't. By the time I had made it happen I wouldn't want it."

"That's my trouble too," Gertrude said. Then she turned over on her pillow and sobbed helplessly. "Jimmie had such ducky little curls," she explained incoherently. "I do this sometimes when I think of them. Otherwise, I'm not a crying woman."

Margaret put out a hand to her; but long after Gertrude's breath began to rise and fall regularly, she lay staring wide-eyed into the darkness.

CHAPTER XXI

ELEANOR HEARS THE NEWS

"Dear Uncle Jimmie:

"I said I would write you, but now that I have taken this hour in which to do it, I find it is a very, very hard letter that I have got to write. In the first place I can't believe that the things you said to me that night were real, or that you were awake and in the world of realities when you said them. I felt as if we were both dreaming; that you were talking as a man does sometimes in delirium when he believes the woman he loves to be by his side, and I was listening the same way. It made me very happy, as dreams sometimes do. I can't help feeling that your idea of me is a dream idea, and the pain that you said this kind of a letter would give you will be merely dream pain. It is a shock to wake up in the morning and find that all the lovely ways we felt, and delicately beautiful things we had, were only dream things that we wouldn't even understand if we were thoroughly awake.

"In the second place, you can't want to marry your little niecelet, the funny little 'kiddo,' that used to burn her fingers and the beefsteak over that old studio gas stove. We had such lovely kinds of make-believe together. That's what our association always ought to mean to us,—just chumship, and wonderful and preposterous *pretends*. I couldn't think of myself being married to you any more than I could Jack the giant killer, or Robinson Crusoe. You're my truly best and dearest childhood's playmate, and that is a great deal to be, Uncle Jimmie. I don't think a little girl ever grows up quite *whole* unless she has somewhere, somehow, what I had in you. You wouldn't want to marry Alice in Wonderland, now would you? There are some kinds of playmates that can't marry each other. I think that you and I are that kind, Uncle Jimmie.

"My dear, my dear, don't let this hurt you. How can it hurt you, when I am only your little adopted foster child that you have helped support and comfort and make a beautiful, glad life for? I love you so much,—you are so precious to me that you *must* wake up out of this distorted, though lovely dream that I was present at!

"We must all be happy. Nobody can break our hearts if we are strong enough to withhold them. Nobody can hurt us too much if we can find the way to be our bravest all the time. I know that what you are feeling now is not real. I can't tell you how I know, but I do know the difference. The roots are not deep enough. They could be pulled up without too terrible a havoc.

"Uncle Jimmie, dear, believe me, believe me. I said this would be a hard letter to write, and it has been. If you could see my poor inkstained, weeping face, you would realize that I am only your funny little Eleanor after all, and not to be taken seriously at all. I hope you will come up for my graduation. When you see me with all the other lumps and frumps that are here, you will know that I am not worth considering except as a kind of human joke.

"Good-by, dear, my dear, and God bless you.

"Eleanor."

It was less than a week after this letter to Jimmie that Margaret spending a week-end in a town in Connecticut adjoining that in which Eleanor's school was located, telephoned Eleanor to join her overnight at the inn where she was staying. She had really planned the entire expedition for the purpose of seeing Eleanor and preparing her for the revelations that were in store for her, though she was ostensibly meeting a motoring party, with which she was going on into the Berkshires.

She started in abruptly, as was her way, over the salad and cheese in the low studded Arts and Crafts dining-room of the fashionable road house, contrived to look as self-conscious as a pretty woman in new sporting clothes.

"Your Uncle David and your Uncle Jimmie are going to be married," she told her. "Did you know it, Eleanor?"

"No, I didn't," Eleanor said faintly, but she grew suddenly very white.

"Aren't you surprised, dear? David gave a dinner party one night last week in his studio, and announced his intentions, but we don't know the name of the lady yet, and we can't guess it. He says it is not a society girl."

"Who do you think it is?"

"Who do you think it is, Eleanor?"

"I—I can't think, Aunt Margaret."

"We don't know who Jimmie is marrying either. The facts were merely insinuated, but he said we should have the shock of our lives when we knew."

"When did he tell you?"

"A week ago last Wednesday. I haven't seen him since."

"Perhaps he has changed his mind by now," Eleanor said.

"I don't think that's likely. They were both very much in earnest. Aren't you surprised, Eleanor?"

"I—I don't know. Don't you think it might be that they both just thought they were going to marry somebody—that really doesn't want to marry them? It might be all a mistake, you know."

"I don't think it's a mistake. David doesn't make mistakes."

"He might make one," Eleanor persisted.

Margaret found the rest of her story harder to tell than she had anticipated. Eleanor, wrapped in the formidable aloofness of the sensitive young, was already suffering from the tale she had come to tell,—why, it was not so easy to determine. It might be merely from the pang of being shut out from confidences that she felt should have been shared with her at once.

She waited until they were both ready for bed (their rooms were connecting)—Eleanor in the straight folds of her white dimity nightgown, and her two golden braids making a picture that lingered in Margaret's memory for many years. "It would have been easier to tell her in her street clothes," she thought. "I wish her profile were not so perfect, or her eyes were shallower. How can I hurt such a lovely thing?"

"Are the ten Hutchinsons all right?" Eleanor was asking.

"The ten Hutchinsons are very much all right. They like me better now that I have grown a nice hard Hutchinson shell that doesn't show my feelings through. Haven't you noticed how much more like other people I've grown, Eleanor?"

"You've grown nicer, and dearer and sweeter, but I don't think you're very much like anybody else, Aunt Margaret."

"I have though,—every one notices it. You haven't asked me anything about Peter yet," she added suddenly.

The lovely color glowed in Eleanor's cheeks for an instant.

"Is—is Uncle Peter well?" she asked. "I haven't heard from him for a long time."

"Yes, he's well," Margaret said. "He's looking better than he was for a while. He had some news to tell us too, Eleanor."

Eleanor put her hand to her throat.

"What kind of news?" she asked huskily.

"He's going to be married too. It came out when the others told us. He said that he hadn't the consent of the lady to mention her name yet. We're as much puzzled about him as we are about the other two."

"It's Aunt Beulah," Eleanor said. "It's Aunt Beulah."

She sat upright on the edge of the bed and stared straight ahead of her. Margaret watched the light and life and youth die out of the face and a pitiful ashen pallor overspread it.

"I don't think it's Beulah," Margaret said. "Beulah knows who it is, but I never thought of it's being Beulah herself."

"If she knows—then she's the one. He wouldn't have told her first if she hadn't been."

"Don't let it hurt you too much, dear. We're all hurt some, you know. Gertrude—and me, too, Eleanor. It's—it's pain to us all."

"Do you mean—Uncle David, Aunt Margaret?"

"Yes, dear," Margaret smiled at her bravely.

"And does Aunt Gertrude care about Uncle Jimmie?"

"She has for a good many years, I think."

Eleanor covered her face with her hands.

"I didn't know that," she said. "I wish somebody had told me." She pushed Margaret's arm away from her gently, but her breath came hard. "Don't touch me," she cried, "I can't bear it. You might not want to—if you knew. Please go,—oh! please go—oh! please go."

As Margaret closed the door gently between them, she saw Eleanor throw her head back, and push the back of her hand hard against her mouth, as if to stifle the rising cry of her anguish.

The next morning Eleanor was gone. Margaret had listened for hours in the night but had heard not so much as the rustle of a garment from the room beyond. Toward morning she had fallen into the sleep of exhaustion. It was then that the stricken child had made her escape. "Miss Hamlin had found that she must take the early train," the clerk said, "and left this note for Miss Hutchinson." It was like Eleanor to do things decently and in order.

"Dear Aunt Margaret," her letter ran. "My grandmother used to say that some people were trouble breeders. On thinking it over I am afraid that is just about what I am,—a trouble breeder.

"I've been a worry and bother and care to you all since the beginning, and I have repaid all your kindness by bringing trouble upon you. Perhaps you can guess what I mean. I don't think I have any right to tell you exactly in this letter. I can only pray that it will be found to be all a mistake, and come out right in the end. Surely such beautiful people as you and Uncle David can find the way to each other, and can help Uncle Jimmie and Aunt Gertrude, who are a little blinder about life. Surely, when the stumbling block is out of the way, you four will walk together beautifully. Please try, Aunt Margaret, to make things as right as if I had never helped them to go wrong. I was so young, I didn't know how to manage. I shall never be that kind of young again. I grew up last night, Aunt Margaret.

"You know the other reason why I am going. Please do not let any one else know. If the others could think I had met with some accident, don't you think that would be the wisest way? I would like to arrange it so they wouldn't try to find me at all, but would just mourn for me naturally for a little while. I thought of sticking my old cap in the river, but I was afraid that would be too hard for you. There won't be any use in trying to find me. I am going where you can not. I couldn't ever bear seeing one of your faces again. I have done too much harm. Don't let Uncle Peter *know*, please, Aunt Margaret. I don't want him to know,—I don't want to hurt him, and I don't want him to know.

"Oh! I have loved you all so much. Good-by, my dears, my dearests. I have taken all of my allowance money. Please forgive me.

"Eleanor."

CHAPTER XXII

THE SEARCH

Eleanor had not bought a ticket at the station, Margaret ascertained, but the ticket agent had tried to persuade her to. She had thanked him and told him that she preferred to buy it of the conductor. He was a lank, saturnine individual and had been seriously smitten with Eleanor's charms, it appeared, and the extreme solicitousness of his attitude at the suggestion of any mystery connected with her departure made Margaret realize the caution with which it would be politic to proceed. She had very little hope of finding Eleanor back at the school, but it was still rather a shock when she telephoned the school office and found that there was no news of her there. She concocted a somewhat lame story to account for Eleanor's absence and promised the authorities that she would be sent back to them within the week,—a promise she was subsequently obliged to acknowledge that she could not keep. Then she fled to New York to break the disastrous news to the others.

She told Gertrude the truth and showed her the pitiful letter Eleanor had left behind her, and together they wept over it. Also together, they faced David and Jimmie.

"She went away," Margaret told them, "both because she felt she was hurting those that she loved and because she herself was hurt."

"What do you mean?" David asked.

"I mean—that she belonged body and soul to Peter and to nobody else," Margaret answered deliberately.

David bowed his head. Then he threw it back again, suddenly.

"If that is true," he said, "then I am largely responsible for her going."

"It is I who am responsible," Jimmie groaned aloud. "I asked her to marry me and she refused me."

"I asked her to marry me and didn't give her the chance to refuse," David said; "it is that she is running away from."

"It was Peter's engagement that was the last straw," Margaret said. "The poor baby withered and shrank like a flower in the blast when I told her that."

"The damned hound—" Jimmie said feelingly and without apology. "Who's he engaged to anyway?"

"Eleanor says it's Beulah, and the more I think of it the more I think that she's probably right."

"That would be a nice mess, wouldn't it?" Gertrude suggested. "Remember how frank we were with her about his probable lack of judgment, Margaret? I don't covet the sweet job of breaking it to either one of them."

Nevertheless she assisted Margaret to break it to them both late that same afternoon at Beulah's apartment.

"I'll find her," Peter said briefly. And in response to the halting explanation of her disappearance that Margaret and Gertrude had done their best to try to make plausible, despite its elliptical nature, he only said, "I don't see that it makes any difference why she's gone. She's gone, that's the thing that's important. No matter how hard we try we can't really figure out her reason till we find her."

"Are you sure it's going to be so easy?" Gertrude asked. "I mean—finding her. She's a pretty determined little person when she makes up her mind. Eleanor's threats are to be taken seriously. She always makes good on them."

"I'll find her if she's anywhere in the world," Peter said. "I'll find her and bring her back."

Margaret put out her hand to him.

"I believe that you will," she said. "Find out the reason that she went away, too, Peter."

Beulah pulled Gertrude aside.

"It wasn't Peter, was it?" she asked piteously. "She had some one else on her mind, hadn't she?"

"She had something else on her mind," Gertrude answered gravely, "but she had Peter on her mind, too."

"She didn't—she couldn't have known about us—Peter and me. We—we haven't told any one."

"She guessed it, Beulah. She couldn't bear it. Nobody's to blame. It's just one of God's most satirical mix-ups."

"I was to blame," Beulah said slowly. "I don't believe in shifting responsibility. I got her here in the first place and I've been instrumental in guiding her life ever since. Now, I've sacrificed her to my own happiness."

"It isn't so simple as that," Gertrude said; "the things we start going soon pass out of our hands. Somebody a good deal higher up has been directing Eleanor's affairs for a long time,—and ours too, for that matter."

"Don't worry, Beulah," Peter said, making his way to her side from the other corner of the room where he had been talking to Margaret. "You mustn't let this worry you. We've all got to be—soldiers now,—but we'll soon have her back again, I promise you."

"And I promise you," Beulah said chokingly, "that if you'll get her back again, I—I will be a soldier."

Peter began by visiting the business schools in New York and finding out the names of the pupils registered there. Eleanor had clung firmly to her idea of becoming an editorial stenographer in some magazine office, no matter how hard he had worked to dissuade her. He felt almost certain she would follow out that purpose now. There was a fund in her name started some years before for the defraying of her college expenses. She would use that, he argued, to get herself started, even though she felt constrained to pay it back later on. He worked on this theory for some time, even making a trip to Boston in search for her in the stenography classes there, but nothing came of it.

Among Eleanor's effects sent on from the school was a little red address book containing the names and addresses of many of her former schoolmates at Harmon. Peter wrote all the girls he remembered hearing her speak affectionately of, but not one of them was able to give him any news of her. He wrote to Colhassett to Albertina's aunt, who had served in the capacity of housekeeper to Eleanor's grandfather in his last days, and got in reply a pious letter from Albertina herself, who intimated that she had always suspected that Eleanor would come to some bad end, and that now she was highly soothed and gratified by the apparent fulfillment of her sinister prognostications.

Later he tried private detectives, and, not content with their efforts, he followed them over the ground that they covered, searching through boarding houses, and public classes of all kinds; canvassing the editorial offices of the various magazines Eleanor had admired in the hope of discovering that she had applied for some small position there; following every clue that his imagination, and the acumen of the professionals in his service, could supply;—but his patient search was unrewarded. Eleanor had apparently vanished from the surface of the earth. The quest which had seemed to him so simple a matter when he first undertook it, now began to assume terrible and abortive proportions. It was unthinkable that one little slip of a girl untraveled and inexperienced should be able permanently to elude six determined and worldly adult New Yorkers, who were prepared to tax their resources to the utmost in the effort to find her,—but the fact remained that she was missing and continued to be missing, and the cruel month went by and brought them no news of her.

The six guardians took their trouble hard. Apart from the emotions that had been precipitated by her developing charms, they loved her dearly as the child they had taken to their hearts and bestowed all their young enthusiasm and energy and tenderness upon. She was the living clay, as Gertrude had said so many years before, that they had molded as nearly as possible to their hearts' desire. They loved her for herself, but one and all they loved her for what they had made of her—an exquisite, lovely young creature, at ease in a world that might so easily have crushed her utterly if they had not intervened for her.

They kept up the search unremittingly, following false leads and meeting with heartbreaking discouragements and disappointments. Only Margaret had any sense of peace about her.

"I'm sure she's all right," she said; "I feel it. It's hard having her gone, but I'm not afraid for her. She'll work it out better than we could help her to. It's a beautiful thing to be young and strong and free, and she'll get the beauty out of it."

"I think perhaps you're right, Margaret," David said. "You almost always are. It's the bread and butter end of the problem that worries me."

Margaret smiled at him quaintly.

"The Lord provides," she said. "He'll provide for our ewe lamb, I'm sure."

"You speak as if you had it on direct authority."

"I think perhaps I have," she said gravely.

Jimmie and Gertrude grew closer together as the weeks passed, and the strain of their fruitless quest continued. One day Jimmie showed her the letter that Eleanor had written him.

"Sweet, isn't she?" he said, as Gertrude returned it to him, smiling through her tears.

"She's a darling," Gertrude said fervently. "Did she hurt you so much, Jimmie dear?"

"I wanted her," Jimmie answered slowly, "but I think it was because I thought she was mine,—that I could make her mine. When I found she was Peter's,—had been Peter's all the time, the thought somehow cured me. She was dead right, you know. I made it up out of the stuff that dreams are made of. God knows I love her, but—but that personal thing has gone out of it. She's my little lost child,—or my sister. A man wants his own to be his own, Gertrude."

"Yes, I know."

"My—my real trouble is that I'm at sea again. I thought that I cared,—that I was anchored for good. It's the drifting that plays the deuce with me. If the thought of that sweet child and the grief at her loss can't hold me, what can? What hope is there for me?"

"I don't know," Gertrude laughed.

"Don't laugh at me. You've always been on to me, Gertrude, too much so to have any respect for me, I guess. You've got your work," he waved his arm at the huge cast under the shadow of which they were sitting, "and all this. You can put all your human longings into it. I'm a poor rudderless creature without any hope or direction." He buried his face in his hands. "You don't know it," he said, with an effort to conceal the fact that his shoulders were shaking, "but you see before you a human soul in the actual process of dissolution."

Gertrude crossed her studio floor to kneel down beside him. She drew the boyish head, rumpled into an irresistible state of curliness, to her breast.

"Put it here where it belongs," she said softly.

"Do you mean it?" he whispered. "Sure thing? Hope to die? Cross your heart?"

"Yes, my dear."

"Praise the Lord."

"I snitched him," Gertrude confided to Margaret some days later,—her whole being radiant and transfigured with happiness. "You snitch David."

CHAPTER XXIII

The Young Nurse

The local hospital of the village of Harmonville, which was ten miles from Harmon proper, where the famous boarding-school for young ladies was located, presented an aspect so far from institutional that but for the sign board tacked modestly to an elm tree just beyond the break in the hedge that constituted the main entrance, the gracious, old colonial structure might have been taken for the private residence for which it had served so many years.

It was a crisp day in late September, and a pale yellow sun was spread thin over the carpet of yellow leaves with which the wide lawn was covered. In the upper corridor of the west wing, grouped about the window-seat with their embroidery or knitting, the young nurses were talking together in low tones during the hour of the patients' siestas. The two graduates, dark-eyed efficient girls, with skilled delicate fingers taking precise stitches in the needlework before them, were in full uniform, but the younger girls clustered about them, beginners for the most part, but a few months in training, were dressed in the simple blue print, and little white caps and aprons, of the probationary period.

The atmosphere was very quiet and peaceful. A light breeze blew in at the window and stirred a straying lock or two that escaped the starched band of a confining cap. Outside the stinging whistle of the insect world was interrupted now and then by the cough of a passing motor. From the doors opening on the corridor an occasional restless moan indicated the inability of some sufferer to take his dose of oblivion according to schedule. Presently a bell tinkled a summons to the patient in the first room on the right—a gentle little old lady who had just had her appendix removed.

"Will you take that, Miss Hamlin?" the nurse in charge of the case asked the tallest and fairest of the young assistants.

"Certainly." Eleanor, demure in cap and kerchief as the most ravishing of young Priscillas, rose obediently at the request. "May I read to her a little if she wants me to?"

"Yes, if you keep the door closed. I think most of the others are sleeping."

The little old lady who had just had her appendix out, smiled weakly up at Eleanor.

"I hoped 'twould be you," she said, "and then after I'd rung I lay in fear and trembling lest one o' them young flipperti-gibbets should come, and get me all worked up while she was trying to shift me. I want to be turned the least little mite on my left side."

"That's better, isn't it?" Eleanor asked, as she made the adjustment.

"I dunno whether that's better, or whether it just seems better to me, because 'twas you that fixed me," the little old lady said. "You certainly have got a soothin' and comfortin' way with you."

"I used to take care of my grandmother years ago, and the more hospital work I do, the more it comes back to me,—and the better I remember the things that she liked to have done for her."

"There's nobody like your own kith and kin," the little old lady sighed. "There's none left of mine. That other nurse—that black haired one—she said you was an orphan, alone in the world. Well, I pity a young girl alone in the world."

"It's all right to be alone in the world—if you just keep busy enough," Eleanor said. "But you mustn't talk any more. I'm going to give you your medicine and then sit here and read to you."

On the morning of her flight from the inn, after a night spent staring motionless into the darkness, Eleanor took the train to the town some dozen miles beyond Harmonville, where her old friend Bertha Stephens lived. To "Stevie," to whom the duplicity of Maggie Lou had served to draw her very close in the ensuing year, she told a part of her story. It was through the influence of Mrs. Stephens, whose husband was on the board of directors of the Harmonville hospital, that Eleanor had been admitted there. She had resolutely put all her old life behind her. The plan to take up a course in stenography and enter an editorial office was to have been, as a matter of course, a part of her life closely associated with Peter. Losing him, there was nothing left of her dream of high adventure and conquest. There was merely the hurt desire to hide herself where she need never trouble him again, and where she could be independent and useful. Having no idea of her own value to her guardians, or the integral tenderness in which she was held, she sincerely believed that her disappearance must have relieved them of much chagrin and embarrassment.

Her hospital training kept her mercifully busy. She had the temperament that finds a virtue in the day's work, and a balm in its mere iterative quality. Her sympathy and intelligence made her a good nurse and her adaptability, combined with her loveliness, a general favorite.

She spent her days off at the Stephens' home. Bertha Stephens had been the one girl that Peter had failed to write to, when he began to circulate his letters of inquiry. Her name had been set down in the little red book, but he remembered the trouble that Maggie Lou had precipitated, and arrived at the conclusion that the intimacy existing between Eleanor and Bertha had not survived it. Except that Carlo Stephens persisted in trying to make love to her, and Mrs. Stephens covertly encouraged his doing so, Eleanor found the Stephens' home a very comforting haven. Bertha had developed into a full breasted, motherly looking girl, passionately interested in all vicarious love-affairs, though quickly intimidated at the thought of having any of her own. She was devoted to Eleanor, and mothered her clumsily.

It was still to her diary that Eleanor turned for the relief and solace of self-expression.

"It is five months to-day," she wrote, "since I came to the hospital. It seems like five years. I like it, but I feel like the little old woman on the King's Highway. I doubt more every minute if this can be I. Sometimes I wonder what 'being I' consists of, anyway. I used to feel as if I were divided up into six parts as separate as protoplasmic cells, and that each one was looked out for by a different cooperative parent. I thought that I would truly be I when I got them all together, and looked out for them myself, but I find I am no more of an entity than I ever was. The puzzling question of 'what am I?' still persists, and I am farther away from the right answer than ever. Would a sound be a sound if there were no one to hear it? If the waves of vibration struck no human ear, would the sound be in existence at all? This is the problem propounded by one of the nurses yesterday.

"How much of us lives when we are entirely shut out of the consciousness of those whom we love? If there is no one to *realize* us day by day,—if all that love has made of us is taken away, what is left? Is there anything? I don't know. I look in the glass, and see the same face,—Eleanor Hamlin, almost nineteen, with the same bow shaped eyebrows, and the same double ridge leading up from her nose to her mouth, making her look still very babyish. I pinch myself, and find that it hurts just the same as it used to six months ago, but there the resemblance to what I used to be, stops. I'm a young nurse now in hospital training, and very good at it, too, if I do say it as shouldn't; but that's all I am. Otherwise, I'm not anybody *to* anybody,—except a figure of romance to good old Stevie, who doesn't count in this kind of reckoning. I take naturally to nursing they tell me. A nurse is a kind of maternal automaton. I'm glad I'm that, but there used to be a lot more of me than that. There ought to be some heart and brain and soul left over, but there doesn't seem to be. Perhaps I am like the Princess in the fairy story whose heart was an auk's egg. Nobody had power to make her feel unless they reached it and squeezed it.

"I feel sometimes as if I were dead. I wish I could know whether Uncle Peter and Aunt Beulah were married yet. I wish I could know that. There is a woman in this hospital whose suitor married some one else, and she has nervous prostration, and melancholia. All she does all day is to moan and wring her hands and call out his name. The nurses are not very sympathetic. They seem to think that it is disgraceful to love a man so much that your whole life stops as soon as he goes out of it. What of Juliet and Ophelia and Francesca de Rimini? They loved so they could not tear their love out of their hearts without lacerating them forever. There is that kind of love in the world,—bigger than life itself. All the big tragedies of literature were made from it,—why haven't people more sympathy for it? Why isn't there more dignity about it in the eyes of the world?

"It is very unlucky to love, and to lose that which you cherish, but it is unluckier still never to know the meaning of love, or to find 'Him whom your soul loveth.' I try to be kind to that poor forsaken woman. I am sorry for his sake that she calls out his name, but she seems to be in such torture of mind and body that she is unable to help it.

"They are trying to cut down expenses here, so they have no regular cook, the housekeeper and her helper are supposed to do it all. I said I would make the desserts, so now I have got to go down-stairs and make some fruit gelatin. It is best that I should not write any more to-day, anyway."

Later, after the Thanksgiving holiday, she wrote:

"I saw a little boy butchered to-day, and I shall never forget it. It is wicked to speak of Doctor Blake's clean cut work as butchery, but when you actually see a child's leg severed from its body, what else can you call it?

"The reason that I am able to go through operations without fainting or crying is just this: *other people do*. The first time I stood by the operating table to pass the sterilized instruments to the assisting nurse, and saw the half naked doctors hung in rubber standing there preparing to carve their way through the naked flesh of the unconscious creature before them, I felt the kind of pang pass through my heart that seems to kill as it comes. I thought I died, or was dying,—and then I looked up and saw that every one else was ready for their work. So I drew a deep breath and became ready too. I don't think there is anything in the world too hard to do if you look at it that way.

"The little boy loved me and I loved him. We had hoped against hope that we would be able to save his poor little leg, but it had to go. I held his hand while they gave him the chloroform. At his head sat Doctor Hathaway with his Christlike face, draped in the robe of the anesthetist. 'Take long breaths, Benny,' I said, and he breathed in bravely. It was over quickly. To-morrow, when he is really out of the ether, I have got to tell him what was done to him. Something happened to me while that operation was going on. He hasn't any mother. I think the spirit of the one who was his mother passed into me, and I knew what it would be like to be the mother of a son. Benny was not without what his mother would have felt for him if she had been at his side. I can't explain it, but that is what I felt.

"To-night it is as black as ink outside. There are no stars. I feel as if there should be no stars. If there were, there might be some strange little bit of comfort in them that I could cling to. I do not want any comfort from outside to shine upon me to-night. I have got to draw all my strength from a source within, and I feel it welling up within me even now.

"I wonder if I have been selfish to leave the people I love so long without any word of me. I think Aunt Gertrude and Aunt Beulah and Aunt Margaret all had a mother feeling for me. I am remembering to-night how anxious they used to be for me to have warm clothing, and to keep my feet dry, and not to work too hard at school. All those things that I took as a matter of course, I realize now were very significant and beautiful. If I had a child and did not know to-night where it would lie down to sleep, or on what pillow it would put its head, I know my own rest would be troubled. I wonder if I have caused any one of my dear mothers to feel like that. If I have, it has been very wicked and cruel of me."

CHAPTER XXIV

CHRISTMAS AGAIN

The ten Hutchinsons having left the library entirely alone in the hour before dinner, David and Margaret had appropriated it and were sitting companionably together on the big couch drawn up before the fireplace, where a log was trying to consume itself unscientifically head first.

"I would stay to dinner if urged," David suggested.

"You stay," Margaret agreed laconically.

She moved away from him, relaxing rather limply in the corner of the couch, with a hand dangling over the farther edge of it.

"You're an inconsistent being," David said. "You buoy all the rest of us up with your faith in the well-being of our child, and then you pine yourself sick over her absence."

"It's Christmas coming on. We always had such a beautiful time on Christmas. It was so much fun buying her presents. It isn't like Christmas at all with her gone from us."

"Do you remember how crazy she was over the ivory set?"

"And the bracelet watch?"

"Do you remember the Juliet costume?" David's eyes kindled at the reminiscence. "How wonderful she was in it."

Margaret drew her feet up on the couch suddenly, and clasped her hands about her knees. David laughed.

"I haven't seen you do that for years," he said.

"What?"

"Hump yourself in that cryptic way."

"Haven't you?" she said. "I was just wondering—" but she stopped herself suddenly.

"Wondering what?" David was watching her narrowly, and perceiving it, she flushed.

"This is not my idea of an interesting conversation," she said; "it's getting too personal."

"I can remember the time when you told me that you didn't find things interesting unless they were personal. 'I like things very personal,' you said— in those words."

"I did then."

"What has changed you?" David asked gravely.

"The chill wind of the world, I guess; the most personal part of me is frozen stiff."

"I never saw a warmer creature in my life," David protested. "On that same occasion you said that being a woman was about like being a field of clover in an insectless world. You don't feel that way nowadays, surely,—at the rate the insects have been buzzing around you this winter. I've counted at least seven, three bees, one or two beetles, a butterfly and a worm."

"I didn't know you paid that much attention to my poor affairs."

"I do, though. If you hadn't put your foot down firmly on the worm, I had every intention of doing so."

"Had you?"

"I had."

"On that occasion to which you refer I remember I also said that I had a queer hunch about Eleanor."

"Margaret, are you deliberately changing the subject?"

"I am."

"Then I shall bring the butterfly up later."

"I said," Margaret ignored his interruption, "that I had the feeling that she was going to be a storm center and bring some kind of queer trouble upon us."

"Yes."

"She did, didn't she?"

"I'm not so sure that's the way to put it," David said gravely. "We brought queer trouble on her."

"She made—you—suffer."

"She gave my vanity the worst blow it has ever had in its life," David corrected her. "Look here, Margaret, I want you to know the truth about that. I—I stumbled into that, you know. She was so sweet, and before I knew it I had—I found myself in the attitude of making love to her. Well, there was nothing to do but go through with it. I wanted to, of course. I felt like Pygmalion—but it was all potential, unrealized—and ass that I was, I assumed that she would have no other idea in the matter. I was going to marry her because I—I had started things going, you know. I had no choice even if I had wanted one. It never occurred to me that she might have a choice, and so I went on trying to make things easy for her, and getting them more tangled at every turn."

"You never really—cared?" Margaret's face was in shadow.

"Never got the chance to find out. With characteristic idiocy I was keeping out of the picture until the time was ripe. She really ran away to get away from the situation I created and she was quite right too. If I weren't haunted by these continual pictures of our offspring in the bread line, I should be rather glad than otherwise that she's shaken us all till we get our breath back. Poor Peter is the one who is smashed, though. He hasn't smiled since she went away."

"You wouldn't smile if you were engaged to Beulah."

"Are they still engaged?"

"Beulah has her ring, but I notice she doesn't wear it often."

"Jimmie and Gertrude seem happy."

"They are, gloriously."

"That leaves only us two," David suggested. "Margaret, dear, do you think the time will ever come when I shall get you back again?"

Margaret turned a little pale, but she met his look steadily.

"Did you ever lose me?"

"The answer to that is 'yes,' as you very well know. Time was when we were very close—you and I, then somehow we lost the way to each other. I'm beginning to realize that it hasn't been the same world since and isn't likely to be unless you come back to me."

"Was it I who strayed?"

"It was I; but it was you who put the bars up and have kept them there."

"Was I to let the bars down and wait at the gate?"

"If need be. It should be that way between us, Margaret, shouldn't it?"

"I don't know," Margaret said, "I don't know." She flashed a sudden odd look at him. "If—when I put the bars down, I shall run for my life. I give you warning, David."

"Warning is all I want," David said contentedly. He could barely reach her hand across the intervening expanse of leather couch, but he accomplished it,—he was too wise to move closer to her. "You're a lovely, lovely being," he said reverently. "God grant I may reach you and hold you."

She curled a warm little finger about his.

"What would Mrs. Bolling say?" she asked practically.

"To tell you the truth, she spoke of it the other day. I told her the Eleanor story, and that rather brought her to her senses. She wouldn't have liked that, you know; but now all the eligible buds are plucked, and she wants me to settle down."

"Does she think I'm a settling kind of person?"

"She wouldn't if she knew the way you go to my head," David murmured. "Oh, she thinks that you'll do. She likes the ten Hutchinsons."

"Maybe I'd like them better considered as connections of yours," Margaret said abstractedly.

David lifted the warm little finger to his lips and kissed it swiftly.

"Where are you going?" he asked, as she slipped away from him and stood poised in the doorway.

"I'm going to put on something appropriate to the occasion," she answered.

When she came back to him she was wearing the most delicate and cobwebby of muslins with a design of pale purple passion flowers trellised all over it, and she gave him no chance for a moment alone with her all the rest of the evening.

Sometime later she showed him Eleanor's parting letter, and he was profoundly touched by the pathetic little document.

As the holidays approached Eleanor's absence became an almost unendurable distress to them all. The annual Christmas dinner party, a function that had never been omitted since the acquisition of David's studio, was decided on conditionally, given up, and again decided on.

"We do want to see one another on Christmas day,—we've got presents for one another, and Eleanor would hate it if she thought that her going away had settled that big a cloud on us. She slipped out of our lives in order to bring us closer together. We'll get closer together for her sake," Margaret decided.

But the ordeal of the dinner itself was almost more than they had reckoned on. Every detail of traditional ceremony was observed even to the mound of presents marked with each name piled on the same spot on the couch, to be opened with the serving of the coffee.

"I got something for Eleanor," Jimmie remarked shamefacedly as he added his contributions to the collection. "Thought we could keep it for her, or throw it into the waste-basket or something. Anyhow I had to get it."

"I guess everybody else got her something, too," Margaret said. "Of course we will keep them for her. I got her a little French party coat. It will be just as good next year as this. Anyhow as Jimmie says, I had to get it."

"I got her slipper buckles," Gertrude admitted. "She has always wanted them."

"I got her the Temple *Shakespeare*," Beulah added. "She was always carrying around those big volumes."

"You're looking better, Beulah," Margaret said. "Are you feeling better?"

"Jimmie says I'm looking more human. I guess perhaps that's it,—I'm feeling more—human. I needed humanizing—even at the expense of some—some heartbreak," she said bravely.

Margaret crossed the room to take a seat on Beulah's chair-arm, and slipped an arm around her.

"You're all right if you know that," she whispered softly.

"I thought I was going to bring you Eleanor herself," Peter said. "I got on the trail of a girl working in a candy shop out in Yonkers. My faithful sleuth was sure it was Eleanor and I was ass enough to believe he knew what he was talking about. When I got out there I found a strawberry blonde with gold teeth."

"Gosh, you don't think she's doing anything like that," Jimmie exclaimed.

"I don't know," Peter said miserably. He was looking ill and unlike himself. His deep set gray eyes were sunken far in his head, his brow was too white, and the skin drawn too tightly over his jaws. "As a de-tec-i-tive, I'm afraid I'm a failure."

"We're all failures for that matter," David said. "Let's have dinner."

Eleanor's empty place, set with the liqueur glass she always drank her thimbleful of champagne in, and the throne chair from the drawing-room in which she presided over the feasts given in her honor, was almost too much for them. Margaret cried openly over her soup. Peter shaded his eyes with his hand, and Gertrude and Jimmie groped for each other's hands under the shelter of the table-cloth.

"This—this won't do," David said. He turned to Beulah on his left, sitting immovable, with her eyes staring unseeingly into the centerpiece of holly and mistletoe arranged by Alphonse so lovingly. "We must either turn this into a kind of a wake, and kneel as we feast, or we must try to rise above it somehow."

"I don't see why," Jimmie argued. "I'm in favor of each man howling informally as he listeth."

"Let's drink her health anyhow," David insisted. "I cut out the Sauterne and the claret, so we could begin on the wine at once in this contingency. Here's to our beloved and dear absent daughter."

"Long may she wave," Jimmie cried, stumbling to his feet an instant after the others.

While they were still standing with their glasses uplifted, the bell rang.

"Don't let anybody in, Alphonse," David admonished him.

They all turned in the direction of the hall, but there was no sound of parley at the front door. Eleanor had put a warning finger to her lips, as Alphonse opened it to find her standing there. She stripped off her hat and her coat as she passed through the drawing-room, and stood in her little blue cloth traveling dress between the portières that separated it from the dining-room. The six stood transfixed at the sight of her, not believing the vision of their eyes.

"You're drinking my health," she cried, as she stretched out her arms to them. "Oh! my dears, and my dearest, will you forgive me for running away from you?"

CHAPTER XXV

THE LOVER

They left her alone with Peter in the drawing room in the interval before the coffee, seeing that he had barely spoken to her though his eyes had not left her face since the moment of her spectacular appearance between the portières.

"I'm not going to marry you, Peter," Beulah whispered, as she slipped by him to the door, "don't think of me. Think of her."

But Peter was almost past coherent thought or speech as they stood facing each other on the hearth-rug,—Eleanor's little head up and her breath coming lightly between her sweet, parted lips.

"Where did you go?" Peter groaned. "How could you, dear—how could you,—how could you?"

"I'm back all safe, now, Uncle Peter. I took up nursing in a hospital."

"I didn't even find you. I swore that I would. I've searched for you everywhere."

"I'm sorry I made you all that trouble," Eleanor said, "but I thought it would be the best thing to do."

"Tell me why," Peter said, "tell me why, I've suffered so much—wondering—wondering."

"You've suffered?" Eleanor cried. "I thought it was only I who did the suffering."

She moved a step nearer to him, and Peter gripped her hard by the shoulders.

"It wasn't that you cared?" he said. Then his lips met hers dumbly, beseechingly.

"It was all a mistake,—my going away," she wrote some days after. "I ought to have stayed at the school, and graduated, and then come down to New York, and faced things. I have my lesson now about facing things. If any other crisis comes into my life, I hope I shall be as strong as Dante was, when he 'showed himself more furnished with breath than he was,' and said, 'Go on, for I am strong and resolute.' I think we always have more strength than we understand ourselves to have.

"I am so wonderfully happy about Uncle David and Aunt Margaret, and I know Uncle Jimmie needs Aunt Gertrude and has always needed her. Did my going away help those things to their fruition? I hope so.

"I can not bear to think of Aunt Beulah, but I know that I must bear to think of her, and face the pain of having hurt her as I must face every other thing that comes into my life from this hour. I would give her back Peter, if I could,—but I can not. He is mine, and I am his, and we have been that way from the beginning. I have thought of him always as stronger and wiser than any one in the world, but I don't think he is. He has suffered and stumbled along, trying blindly to do right, hurting Aunt Beulah and mixing up his life like any man, just the way Uncle Jimmie and Uncle David did.

"Don't men know who it is they love? They seem so often to be struggling hungrily after the wrong thing, trying to get, or to make themselves take, some woman that they do not really want. When women love it is not like that with them.

"When women love! I think I have loved Peter from the first minute I saw him, so beautiful and dear and sweet, with that *anxious* look in his eyes,—that look of consideration for the other person that is always so much a part of him. He had it the first night I saw him, when Uncle David brought me to show me to my foster parents for the first time. It was the thing I grew up by, and measured men and their attitude to women by—just that look in his eyes, that tender warm look of consideration.

"It means a good many things, I think,—a gentle generous nature, and a tender chivalrous heart. It means selflessness. It means being a good man, and one who *protects* by sheer unselfish instinct. I don't know how I shall ever heal him of the hurt he has done Aunt Beulah. Aunt Margaret tells me that Aunt Beulah's experience with him has been the thing that has made her whole, that she needed to live through the human cycle of emotion—of love and possession and renunciation before she could be quite real and sound. This may be true, but it is not the kind of reasoning for Peter and me to comfort ourselves with. If a surgeon makes a mistake in cutting that afterwards does more good than harm, he must not let that result absolve him from his mistake. Nothing can efface the mistake itself, and Peter and I must go on feeling that way about it.

"I want to write something down about my love before I close this book to-night. Something that I can turn to some day and read, or show to my children when love comes to them. 'This is the way I felt,' I want to say to them, 'the first week of my love—this is what it meant to me.'

"It means being a greater, graver, and more beautiful person than you ever thought you could be. It means knowing what you are, and what you were meant to be all at once, and I think it means your chance to be purified for the life you are to live, and the things you are to do in it. Experience teaches, but I think love forecasts and points the way, and shows you what you can be. Even if the light it sheds should grow dim after a while, the path it has shown you should be clear to your inner eye forever and ever. Having been in a great temple is a thing to be better for all your life.

"It means that the soul and the things of the soul are everlasting,—that they have got to be everlasting if love is like this. Love between two people is more than the simple fact of their being drawn together and standing hand in hand. It is the holy truth about the universe. It is the rainbow of God's promise set over the land. There comes with it the soul's certainty of living on and on through time and space.

"Just my loving Peter and Peter's loving me isn't the important thing,—the important thing is the way it has started the truth going; my knowing and understanding mysterious laws that were sealed to me before; Peter taking my life in his hands and making it consecrated and true,—so true that I will not falter or suffer from any misunderstandings or mistaken pain.

"It means warmth and light and tenderness, our love does, and all the poetry in the world, and all the motherliness, (I feel so much like his mother). Peter is my lover. When I say that he is not stronger or wiser than any one in the world I mean—in living. I mean in the way he behaves like a little bewildered boy sometimes. In loving he is stronger and wiser than any living being. He takes my two hands in his and gives me all the strength and all the wisdom and virtue there is in the world.

"I haven't written down anything, after all, that any one could read. My children can't look over my shoulder on to this page, for they would not understand it. It means nothing to any one in the world but me. I shall have to translate for them or I shall have to say to them, 'Children, on looking into this book, I find I can't tell you what love meant to me, because the words I have put down would mean nothing to you. They were only meant to inform me, whenever I should turn back to them, of the great glory and holiness that fell upon me like a garment when love came.'

"And if there should be any doubt in my heart as to the reality of the feeling that has come to them in their turn, I should only have to turn their faces up to the light, and look into their eyes and *know*.

"I shall not die as my own mother did. I know that. I know that Peter will be by my side until we both are old. These facts are established in my consciousness I hardly know how, and I know that they are there,—but if such a thing could be that I should die and leave my little children, I would not be afraid to leave them alone in a world that has been so good to me, under the protection of a Power that provided me with the best and kindest guardians that a little orphan ever had. God bless and keep them all, and make them happy."

THE END